Drawing for Publication

Drawing for Publication
A manual for technical illustrators

Louis Dezart

The Architectural Press : London

First published in 1980 by The Architectural
Press Ltd: London

ISBN 0 85139 185 0 (Cloth)
ISBN 0 85139 184 2 (Paper)

Printed in Great Britain by W T J Mackay Ltd,
Chatham, Kent
using typesetting prepared by Ronset Ltd,
Darwen, Lancs

Contents

Preface and Acknowledgements

It is fairly safe to say that nearly all the draughtsman's output is reproduced in one form or another, and almost as safe to say that the most common form is by *diazo* or other method of same-size reproduction. Since this form of reproduction satisfies the needs of the architectural, engineering, surveying and other professions, the limited time that is spared from their respective courses for instruction in graphics is naturally taken up by the type of drawing suited to their particular requirements. Those who graduate with an aptitude for illustration find themselves specialists in a somewhat narrow field, inasmuch as in the normal course of events they do not have to think about any possible reduction of their drawings. Consequently, if such an event occurs, the draughtsman's thinking is not oriented to the requirements of such drawing and, not surprisingly, some odd results can follow.

The purpose of this book is two-fold. Firstly, to broaden the scope of those who have advanced beyond the student grade by encouraging them to adapt their skills to cover drawings specifically for publication in technical books, magazines, leaflets (and other advertising matter), reports, etc., no matter what specialist discipline is at present being followed. And secondly, by hopefully thus stimulating the mental attitude towards this form of drawing, encouraging the illustrator to present his material as an integral part of the publication, however large or small, and not just accept that it will be regarded simply as space filling.

It is recognised that drawing style is essentially an individual means of expression, influenced and developed, as are so many other skills, by the absorption of ideas and information. The intention here is not to attempt to change an individual style – even if this were necessary – but simply to present the techniques and disciplines which this form of drawing demands in such a way that they may be easily assimilated, whether a definitive drawing style has been developed or not. Where, for example, consistency of style is mentioned in terms of linework and lettering, this relates to the size, weight and density affecting a set or series of illustrations, not a desire to standardise all drawing or influence change.

The content is by no means exhaustive, being intended only to cover the basic principles (and a little beyond) to set the reader on the way and in the right direction. The methods of assessing, preparing and finalising art work are not at all theoretical, but have been used over a period of years by different people for different forms of publication and have proved satisfactory. The order of chapters is not meant to indicate the degree of importance attached to any specific topic – except perhaps for 'Technical Terms', which, for the purposes of communication, should logically be at the beginning. In the absence of any pre-conceived planning, however, the sequence could be used as a rational approach to the appreciation and treatment of draft material.

Finally, there will always be a demand for informative literature, be it book, magazine or catalogue, and equally, therefore, illustrators. It is hoped that those who have not yet entered the publishing field in any form will, after reading the following pages, be encouraged to take the first step.

The production of any book is invariably the result of the work of numerous people, and I would like to express my thanks in particular to

Margaret Crowther, whose original idea set the wheels in motion and who kept them turning; to Gaston, who read and commented on the first draft and Carol, who typed the final version; to Trevor Paulett, who very kindly read the text and made many useful suggestions, and by no means least, to my wife, for her support and tolerance.

Credits

A number of the illustrations used, or were influenced by, products of manufacturers or sources as listed below:

Alfac (Pelltech Limited) Chapter 2, Fig 14; Chapter 5, Figs 10, 12a, 23, 25; Chapter 7, Fig 17

British Standards Institution Chapter 5, Fig 7

Faber–Castell Chapter 7, Fig 11

Geliot Whitman Limited Chapter 2, Fig 3; Chapter 7, Fig 21

Grant Equipment and Supplies Limited Chapter 2, Fig 8

JK Lighting Displays Limited Chapter 2, Figs 7a, 7b

Letraset UK Limited Chapter 2, Fig 14; Chapter 5, Figs 10, 12a, 23, 25; Chapter 7, Figs 17, 19

Linex Chapter 2, Figs 13a, b, c, d

Mecanorma UK Limited Chapter 3, Fig 14; Chapter 5, Figs 10, 12a, 23, 25; Chapter 7, Fig 17

Rabone Chesterman Chapter 2, Figs 4, 5

Standardgraph Sales Co Limited Chapter 5, Fig 9; Chapter 7, Fig 11

UNO Sales Chapter 2, Figs 9, 10; Chapter 7, Figs 11, 12

Zipatone Inc Chapter 2, Fig 14; Chapter 5, Figs 10, 12a, 23, 25; Chapter 7, Fig 17

Introduction

1.1 In common with all other trades and professions, there are words and phrases commonly used by printers and publishers, and which are peculiar to them.

1.2 As the degree of success achieved by any illustrator is to an extent governed by communication, it is obviously desirable that the illustrator should have at least a working knowledge of these terms.

1.3 It is not within the scope of this book to give an exhaustive list – such information can be obtained from books dealing specifically with printing methods and processes. The intention is to restrict the examples to those which the illustrator is likely to meet most frequently and which will enable him or her to communicate freely without time-consuming interpretation or misunderstanding.

1.4 We have included here some terms which are more common to sub-editing and layout; this is because the illustrator will often be working in conjunction with text setting, either drawing to fit a space left or making an allowance for some typesetting.

1.5 Finally, the definitions have been deliberately simplified to avoid a preponderance of yet more technical words and where considered helpful, a diagram has been included to assist the explanation.

Art Paper

A coated paper with a very white surface used for quality-control proofing or reproduction pulls (or copies) of text, tables, illustrations, etc. for photography.

Art Work
A photograph, drawing, sketch, lettering or any combination of these, which is prepared for reproduction.

Ascender
That part of a lower-case letter such as a 'd', 'h', 'k', etc. which extends above the height of the letter 'x'. (Fig **1.1**)

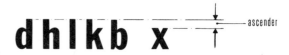

1.1 *Ascender is above the 'x' height*

A/W
Abbreviation for art work.

Bleed
To bleed is to extend the illustration beyond the trimmed allowance for the page so that after trimming the page edge (or edges) forms the border of the illustration.
The bleed is the amount by which the illustration extends beyond the trimmed size to allow for variations in trimming; usually $\frac{1}{8}$ in. (Fig **1.2**)

Block
A relief printing surface of metal produced by photography and chemical etching for letterpress printing. The same term is used for either line or half-tone (*see* letterpress).

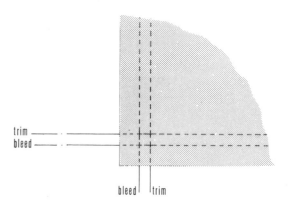

1.2 *Bleed and trim*

Block Pull
A proof of a block to give an idea of the quality which will be obtained when printed. It is usually produced by the blockmaker on coated paper for approval before passing the block on to the printer.

Blow-up
To enlarge any form of art work photographically.

Bold
A typeface with very thick strokes, usually a thickened version of a similar typeface, used to give emphasis to headlines, crossheads, etc. without changing the size of type. (Fig **1.3**)

Bromide
A photographic copy of any illustration usually

1.3 *Bold typeface compared with standard face*

reduced to final size for quality assessment and/ or page layout. Bromides are also used to provide enlarged or reduced copies of original material for use as intermediate drafts.

Camera Copy
Material ready for photography usually for lithographic reproduction. It can consist of any final art work or typesetting or a paste-up combination of both.

Caps
Capitals or upper-case letters. Upper case because type was stored in two containers called cases and mounted one above the other. The capitals were situated in the upper case as distinct from the lower.

Caps and Smalls
Capitals and small capitals (not to be confused with capitals and lower-case), i.e. two sizes of capitals on the same body size in the same fount.

Caption
Wording, preferably set below an illustration, which relates to and specifically describes it. Such wording is usually typeset by the printer, but can be lettered as part of the illustration itself.

Cold Composition
Typesetting by other means than by hot metal casting, such as film setting or typewriter setting.

Condensed.

Continuous Tone
Contact or enlarged print from a photographic negative (*see* half-tone).

Copy
Basic material for printing, such as typescript, photographs etc., which has not yet entered any stage of reproduction.

C. P.

Cropping
Not literally cutting, but changing the size, shape and proportion of an illustration to fit a given space on the layout. This is achieved by

masking the face or placing marks on the back or on an overlay to show what parts are to be omitted (*see* masking).

Depth Scale

A multi-point scale for measuring or setting out lines of type. Usually graduated from 6 pts to 14 pts in $\frac{1}{2}$ pt increments (*see* point).

Descender

That part of a lower-case letter such as the 'g', 'p', 'y', etc., which extends below the foot of the letter 'x'. (Fig 1.4)

1.4 *Descender is below the foot of 'x'*

Didot

The continental system for measuring their own-designed typefaces. The unit is the point as in the Anglo-American system, but is slightly larger, e.g. 12 Didot points measures 0·3 mm more than 12 Anglo-American points (*see* point).

Double-page Spread

A piece of art work designed to extend across a pair of facing pages. (Fig 1.5)

Draft

Author's original sketch or copy for re-drawing.

Dry Transfer

The method by which lettering, symbols and shading patterns can be transferred to art work without the use of any liquid agent but by simply rubbing down.

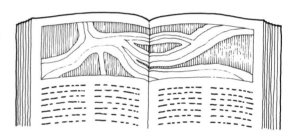

1.5 *Double-page spread*

Electro

A duplicate letterpress printing plate made by electrolytically depositing copper onto a mould taken from the original, and backing with lead alloy.

Em

The square of any size of type, so that a 6 pt em is 6 pts wide and a 10 pt em is 10 pts wide, etc. 12 pt ems (or picas) are used to specify the width of typesetting, columns on a layout page and the width and depth of the type area on a page.

Film Setting
Another name for photo-typesetting.

Font or Fount
A complete collection of all letters, characters, figures, etc. of one size and style of typeface. Serif typefaces have small capitals in addition, while titling founts have no lower-case characters.

Frontis or Frontispiece
Literally the illustration facing the title page, but generally the name given to the introductory or first feature of a magazine.

Full Point
A full stop or period.

Galley Pull or Proof
Originally a proof on a long strip of paper of the metal type which is held in a shallow tray with three raised edges called a galley. The term is in general use for any form of first proof of text no matter how the type is set.

Gatefold
An extra page added to a left or right-hand page to fold out giving in effect a three-page spread. A double gatefold is a fold-out on both left and right-hand pages, giving a four-page spread. (Fig **1.6**)

Gutter
Generally refers to the inner margins of the book that can be used if additional width for an illustration is required, or when a double-page spread is proposed. In reality it is the inner, folded edge, sometimes called the back. (Fig **1.7**)

Half-tone
The process by which greys of various shades from black to white are represented by a pattern of dots of varying sizes. The image is photographed through a screen or grid which breaks up the picture into a pattern of dots. Screens of various gauges can be used to suit the paper on which the half-tone is to be printed. For low quality, absorbent paper, e.g. newsprint, a

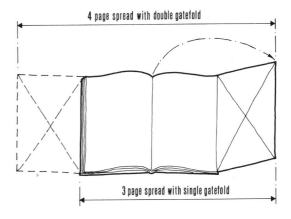

1.6 *Gatefolds*

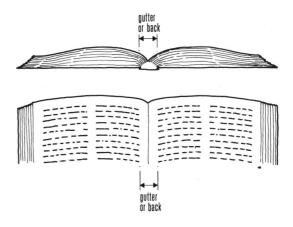

1.7 *Gutter or back*

screen of 60–80 lines per inch would be suitable, while at the other end of the scale, 150 lines per inch could be used for printing on good art paper
(*see* continuous tone).

Hot Metal Setting

Typesetting in which the type is cast from molten metal, as in monotype and linotype setting, as distinguished from filmsetting or typewriter setting.

"IN PRO"

Indent

Beginning a line further in from the margin than the rest of the text setting or positioning an illustration inside the margin of the text. (Fig **1.8**)

Interlinear space.

Italic

The slanted or inclined version of a typeface within a fount. (Fig **1.9**)

Justified

Text set so that the last letter or punctuation mark in each line exactly finishes at the right-hand margin. This is accomplished by varying the spacing between words line by line through-out the setting. (Fig **1.10**)

Keyline

Landscape

Generally used to describe an illustration or material on a page which is turned through 90° so that it reads up the page from the right-hand side. The shape of a book is referred to as land-scape when its width is greater than its height. (Fig **1.11**)

Load. lumps –

Letterpress

The process of printing from a raised surface. The text is cast metal and the illustrations are chemically etched blocks of copper or zinc. (Fig **1.12**)

Light-fast

Not permitting the passage of light. A light-fast material or colour is photographically opaque (*see* photo-opaque).

advantage of being able to conduct experiments within their large housing programme, which has involved:
Development of a 'strategic housing plan' to shorten house completion time
Trying new forms of contract (develop and construct) and encouraging co-operation and partnership within the construction industry
Studies in housing layouts, preferred dwelling plans, and good practice details, to avoid wasteful duplication of design work (this has included pre-packaged working drawings and bills)
Fortunately, the emphasis is now slowly changing from developing building systems and improving the technical design of the elements towards better understanding of the

1.8 *Indented text setting (compare with Fig **1.10**)*

ABCD abcd

1.9 *Italic face (compare with Fig **1.3**)*

that have been placed in the way of private investment in the inner city. They are warned against making 'the best the enemy of the good' in such matters as environmental standards, for industry and planning, generally. Local authorities are urged to bring an area perspective to management. The interaction of housing, environment, social services and employment policies needs to be considered at ground level, instead of as an outcome of some rarified policy discussion at a higher level; and the essential relationship between building decent housing, and maintaining it, and the environment that surrounds it, is drummed home. Attempts will be made to overcome the social

1.10 *Justified text setting (compare with Fig **1.20**)*

Line Shot
A drawing photographed line-for-line in black and white with no greys, as distinct from a half-tone.

Lower Case
Small letters as distinguished from capitals or small capitals. Derived from their location in the lower of the two type-holding cases.

Machine Proof
A good printed copy for checking the quality of illustrations etc. (*see* proof).

Make-up
The laying out of all the component parts of each page – text, illustrations, captions, page numbers, etc. – in their correct positions ready for printing or photography.

Make-ready.

Masking
Indicating the unwanted parts of an illustration or photograph, by using either a light-fast cut-out overlay, opaque tape, marking on a translucent overlay or marking directly on the back.

Measure
The specified width to which a complete line of type is to be set, usually in 12 pt ems (or picas). This is usually, but not always, the maximum width for illustrations.

Offset Litho
A lithographic printing method where the flat image from the printing plate is printed onto an intermediate rubber blanket roller from which it is transferred to the paper (*see* photo lithography).

Original
A photograph or drawing supplied by the author as copy for an illustration, as distinct from a proof or facsimile.

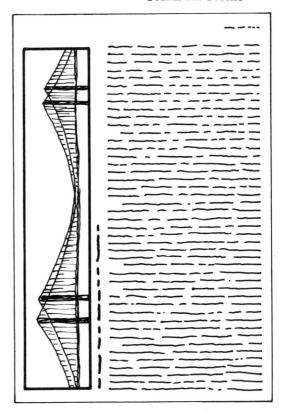

1.11 *Landscaped layout (compare with Fig* **1.16***)*

1.12 *Letterpress printing method*

Overlay

A translucent flap covering the face of, and attached to, a photograph or drawing either for giving instruction for masking, cropping and reproduction generally or to facilitate the adding of tonal differentiation by the photographer.

Ozalid

A method of making photographic copies, particularly paper proofs, from film pages and setting.

Page Proof

A printer's proof of the page as made up, usually on inferior paper, intended to show position of text and pictures rather than quality of printing. For a page on film an ozalid print would be used.

Paste-up

Usually a rough layout using galley proofs of the text and ruled outlines showing the size and position of the illustrations, for use as a guide for the printer to prepare his own make-up. If the paste-up is camera copy, then higher quality text setting and illustration copy would be required and accurate positioning necessary with any further instructions noted in light blue pencil.

Photo Gravure

The process of printing from a recessed surface where the ink is contained in cells of various depths. Gravure half-tone dots, unlike those in other processes, are all the same size, the variation in shade being achieved by the depth of the recess and the amount of ink thereby contained. (Fig **1.13**)

1.13 *Photo gravure printing method*

Photo Lithography

The process of printing from a photographically prepared metal plate on which the flat image attracts the greasy ink while the non-printing areas are protected by a film of water. The commonest printing method is offset lithography using an intermediate blanket roller to prevent the water film transferring to the paper. (Fig **1.14**)

1.14 *Photo lithography printing method*

Photo-opaque

A liquid used to obliterate blemishes on negatives, but in practice is any medium which prevents the passage of light.

Photo-typesetting

Typesetting by photographic means. The resulting output is either photographic paper or transparent film. Proofs will be either the paper itself or ozalid or xerox copies.

Pica

A measurement in the Anglo-American system equalling a 12 pt em, which is about ⅙ of an inch or 4·2 mm. Picas are used to specify the width and depth of type areas irrespective of the size of type in which the page is to be set. The size of illustrations can also be specified in picas where they have to fit in with passages of text.

Point

In typography this is the unit used in sizing type. There are two systems using this unit, each giving it a different value. The continental Didot point is slightly larger at 0·38 mm than the Anglo-American at 0·35 mm. One has to be careful, therefore, when specifying type by point size. For example, 24 pt Univers, being French designed in Didot points, will be larger than 24 pt Franklin Gothic, which is American designed in Anglo-American points. (Fig **1.15**)

Portrait

Generally used to describe illustrations or material on a page where the width is less than the height and their foot is parallel to the bottom of the page. (Fig **1.16**)

Proof

A roughly printed copy for correction and checking, also called a pull (not to be confused with a machine proof).

Range

To align, either left or right, text, headings, notes on drawings, or drawings with text.

1.15 *The point size of type is that measured overall, from the top of the ascender to the bottom of the descender, not just the capital height*

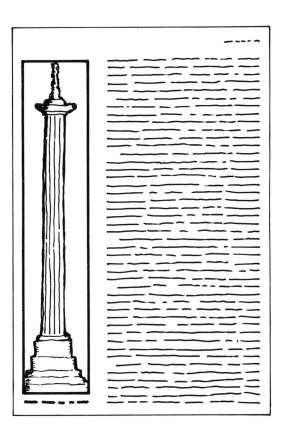

1.16 *Portrait layout*

Reduction

The linear amount by which an illustration is to be photographically reduced before reproduction. The reduction is best expressed as a ratio, e.g. 2:1, 4:1, etc. and it is this factor which has to be applied to lettering size, line thickness, etc. to ensure that the illustration and lettering will be readable after reduction.

Register

The exact alignment of printed pages so that they back each other precisely. Also the accurate superimposition of colours on a multi-colour illustration or of shading tints on a line drawing.

Register Marks

Two (or better, three) marks, often in the form of a cross, to show the relative position and exact orientation of two or more pieces of art work that are to be superimposed. (Fig **1.17**)

1.17 *Some typical register marks*

Repro Pull

Reproduction pull; usually refers to text setting as a high-quality proof on a good art paper for best definition, suitable for photographic reproduction.

Retouching

Hand-work carried out on photographic prints or film to remove blemishes prior to further reproduction. Also applies to the correction of and addition to any hand-prepared art work.

Reverse Left to Right

To reproduce an illustration so as to produce a mirror-like image.

Reverse Out

To reverse black to white when making the final film for a plate or block so that the finished appearance is of white printed on black (or other colour) rather than the normal black on white.

Revise

The revised or second proof after the first has been corrected and returned to the printer.

Roman

Not to be confused with the particular alphabet, but the upright or vertical form of the collection of letters in a fount as distinct from italics.

Rough

The author's sketch or draft or any illustration which will have to be redrawn.

Rontnis -

Sans Serif

Screen

The grid used by the photographer to break down an image into dots for the production of half-tone pictures; or the grade of a dot tint as specified when it is to be applied by the photographer. It is specified in lines-per-inch and, depending upon the quality of paper to be used, can range from 60 (large, coarse dots) to 150 (very small, fine dots) lines-per-inch.

Same Size

Facsimile reproduction with no enlargement or reduction. Also called s/s.

Separation   *Serif*

Set Solid

Lettering or text set so that the line spacing equals the size of the type face used. 18 pt set solid is 18 pt lettering set in lines spaced 18 pts apart. This is the closest line spacing without the ascenders and descenders overlapping. For wide line spacing, type would be specified as, e.g. 8 on 11, i.e. 8 pt type set in lines spaced 11 pts apart. (Fig **1.18**)

Shoot

To photograph with a camera.

Signature

Single Shot

One exposure of the art work to produce one picture. A double shot would be two exposures of the art work to produce one picture.

Sizing

Marking the reduction or the final size required onto an illustration original or working out the final size prior to marking, to assist in the page layout or design.

1.18 (a) *18 pt lettering set solid*

1.18 (b) *8 pt set solid compared with 8 on 11*

Strip-In

To combine two or more pieces of separate art work to form one picture, usually to produce a solid line on a half-tone. Also where one film is cut into another to form a composite image.

Tint

Usually a mechanical tint, i.e. a ready-made dotted, hatched or other pattern printed on film which can be applied direct to art work before photography. Also refers to tonal differentiation applied by hand and a solid panel in a second colour. (Fig **1.19**)

Type Area

The area on a page occupied by text or text and pictures. Sometimes divided into columns, but nevertheless forms the boundaries, top, bottom, left and right, beyond which setting or illustration should not go unless specifically instructed. This area is usually specified in picas (12 pt ems).

Typeface.   Typographic grid

Type Scale

A multi-point scale combined with inches and/or millimetres for measuring widths and depths of pictures and for accurate laying out of material to form pages.

Unjustified

Typesetting where the word spacing is the same line for line so that the right-hand edge is ragged. (Fig **1.20**)

Upper Case

Capital letters.

Widow

The short, last line of a paragraph at the top of a page. Also used to describe the only word of an additional line of text or a note on a drawing. (Fig **1.21**)

X-Height

The height of the lower-case 'x'. Used to define the height of the printing surface of a lower-case alphabet, i.e. a lower-case letter without ascender or descender.

1.19 *Examples of mechanical tints which can be applied to art work by hand*

the boxes and second, laying the slabs. There is an additional work sequence of using temporary staging, needed to dry pack the boxes before the laying of slabs. Site work includes laying services, foundations, connecting the box units together, linking up the services and weather sealing.
The full advantages of prefabrication in the factory are not maximised, because of the site located precast slabs spanning between the boxes; the whole is then clad traditionally by an outer skin of brickwork. In fact, despite the fitting out of the boxes in the factory, this has not yet produced the highest quality interior which factory

1.20 *Unjustified text setting*

This is a masterly guide for the increasing numbers of people going abroad to work and live. The first 60 pages encapsulate advice on job markets available, UK taxation and exchange control (neatly written), letting your home (especially useful), moving house, settling in (shades of bitter experience here), children's education and a comprehensive checklist of conditions of employment.
Two thirds of the book con-

ministries.
There is an excellent index and the whole book is illuminating. By the way: Le Corbusier is quoted once, Jane Jacob once, Oscar Newman eight times and our own Pearl Jephcott eight times; she, of course, knows more about tall buildings and the people who live in them than all the others.
It was interesting to read the book. It is instructive and shows a more positive approach to the

is in charge of the Government review on taxation, recently suggested that the threshold at which VAT becomes payable may be raised from £7500 to £10 000 per annum. Administration of VAT might also be simplified and relief for bad debts allowed.
Corporation tax could be eased by increasing the profit limit before tax becomes operative. Relief from capital gains tax might be allowed where losses ensue from loans to small firms. It has also been suggested that national insurance for the self employed will almost certainly be reduced in April which will also be of benefit to parties in private practice.

1.21 (a) *Widow at top of right-hand column*
      (b) *Widow within a paragraph*

2 Materials and Equipment

Introduction

2.1 Apart from the artistic presentation, the standard of draughtsmanship can only be enhanced by the careful choice of good quality materials and the equipment specifically designed for use with, or on, those materials.

2.2 The scope of the illustrator is generally reflected in his equipment and to an extent the materials upon which he works. The wider the field of operations, the larger should be the 'tool kit' and choice of materials.

2.3 It is important to keep in touch with additions to current ranges of the materials and equipment suppliers. Get on their mailing lists and, through technical representatives, be kept informed of trends and any new developments.

2.4 Always take advantage of samples and trial offers of new aids and materials. A few minutes of practical assessment are worth hours of technical chit-chat and one never knows when such practical experience may come in useful.

Materials

2.5 Contrary perhaps to common belief, it is not at all necessary to prepare art work only on white and fine-surfaced, art, fashion, or other boards.

2.6 The usual method of preparing the photographic intermediate is by means of contrast against a white background rather than by penetration as, for example, diazo copying. This means that any art work prepared on translucent or semi-translucent materials requires a white opaque backing sheet in order to be successfully photographed, but is in no way inferior because of this requirement.

2.7 There is therefore virtually no restriction on the material one can use, apart from any reservations the publisher or printer may have. The prime consideration is whether the art work can be easily prepared and satisfactorily reproduced, so let us look briefly at the materials in common usage which also meet these requirements.

PREPARED AND NATURAL TRACING PAPER

2.8 This is quite suitable for most purposes. It will withstand normal handling, takes erasure reasonably well and, given the correct grade, will produce a satisfactory ink line.

2.9 Choose a medium weight paper, e.g. 90 gm/m^2, with a smooth surface. Although a thin paper is more translucent it will tear easily and make erasure and alteration difficult. A paper with more 'tooth', i.e. with a rough or matt surface will wear pencil and pen points quickly and will not produce an even, dense ink line. (Fig **2.1**) It should be remembered that the camera will only record reflected light and the coarser the material the more it will diffuse the line image. As the surface coarseness increases, so should the spacing of lines and lettering.

2.10 The main disadvantage of this material is its lack of dimensional stability – it cannot be used for accurate overlay purposes, and can also be easily creased and torn if mishandled.

POLYESTER FILM

2.11 This material is highly translucent, durable and dimensionally stable. It is a combination of a clear, shiny, base film which is coated on one or both sides to provide the drawing surface. This surface is quite abrasive and the normal pen and pencil points will wear down very quickly.

2.12 To take full advantage of this material, the smear-proof plastic pencils and tungsten-carbide tipped pens should be used, together with the specially formulated inks produced for use on these films.

a   b

2.1 *Diagrammatic sections showing a 'toothed' or rough surface* (a) *and a smooth surface* (b). *In the case of* (a), *the fine line pen does not produce enough ink to fill and join the cavities to give an even appearance. A much thicker pen has to be employed to achieve this. In* (b) *the fine line ink flow is sufficient*

2.13 Erasures and alterations are easily carried out, the material being capable of withstanding several erasures over the same area without significantly changing its properties.

2.14 Because of its stability and high translucent properties, it is ideal for use where two or more overlays are required to be very accurately registered. Its particular disadvantage is that although it will not tear, it can be easily creased.

TRACING CLOTH

2.15 This was the 'better' drawing medium before the advent of polyester films and still enjoys some popularity. It can be white or blue and the prepared surface will take pencil and ink equally well. The surface can be easily damaged, which makes erasure and subsequent alteration somewhat difficult, but if used with care it will give a very good reproduction image.

2.16 It is more stable than most materials (with the exception of polyester film) but is less translucent, making it ideal for base drawings rather than for overlays. It is perhaps the most expensive of the materials in common use and while it is difficult to tear, it can be very easily creased.

DETAIL PAPER

2.17 This is a semi-translucent material of a predominantly white colour. It is not as versatile as the previously mentioned materials because of its higher degree of opacity, and cannot therefore be used for successive overlays or tracing unless the image beneath is very strong.

2.18 The surface is easily damaged by erasure, and alteration is subsequently difficult to achieve. Because of this, errors should be masked out rather than erased.

2.19 However, because of its white appearance it does give a good contrast to an ink line and this, together with its comparative cheapness, could make it ideal for short-term use – short-term because it does not store too well, being inclined to become brittle with age.

CARTRIDGE PAPER

2.20 This material also gives a good contrast between background and ink line, but the cheaper grades should be avoided as they tend towards a softer surface which makes the ink line less sharp.

2.21 The surface is very easily damaged by erasure, and masking media would be better employed to avoid this. Although it is more substantial than most detail papers, it is not particularly stable and will tear and crease easily.

ILLUSTRATION BOARDS

2.22 These are quite pleasant to work upon and there are many thicknesses and surface finishes from which to choose. They are not cheap, but some of them may well compare favourably with polyester film or tracing cloth.

2.23 Ink and pencil will take equally well and provide a good contrast for photography. They provide a good base for overlay drafting. Erasure can be difficult but the use of masking agents will simplify the correction of errors.

2.24 The thicker boards do not lend themselves easily for use with tee-squares and some drafting machines, where it can be difficult to keep the drawing edge parallel to the surface. (Fig **2.2**)

2.25 The boards do not deteriorate with age, but because of their inflexibility storage of large illustrations could be a problem.

CONCLUSION

2.26 It can be seen that the materials are varied, and because each has qualities suited to different situations, the choice is very largely a personal one.

2.27 You may be lucky (or unlucky) to have the material specified for you by author or publisher. If not, then provided that the method of reproduction can be satisfied, use that material to which you are most accustomed and/or which will suit best the type of illustration to be prepared.

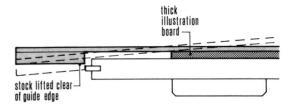

2.2 The thicker boards can cause problems with the drawing edges of tee squares and drafting machines. Use the thinnest possible and protect the edge nearest the stock to avoid friction

2.28 If there is any further doubt as to the choice, remember that the *less* reduction given to an illustration, the *finer* the line must be, and therefore the *smoother* should be the drawing surface.

Equipment

2.29 The most usual items of drawing equipment will be more than just well-known and need not be mentioned here. There are, however, several developments and aids worth commenting on, some of which may be found useful and others essential to this form of illustration.

2.30 As your scope widens, you must be prepared to add to your equipment. Do this as the occasion demands, but be selective. Avoid cluttering yourself up with items that you are only likely to use once or twice a year or those which will save little in time and convenience. Be especially wary of 'aids' that take more time to set up and use than the more traditional methods.

2.31 First, then, to some items with which you should become familiar, starting with the smallest, and then to some of the more useful aids which might well become standard equipment.

2.32 Depth and type scales should be regarded as essential equipment no matter what type or style the illustration may be, since layout grids, sizes of pictures and art work generally will usually be specified in picas or ems.

DEPTH SCALES

2.33 Primarily used for measuring or setting out lines of type or lettering of various sizes and therefore graduated in different point sizes. The scales are available in a variety of forms and materials ranging from a white plastic cut-out with scales of 6 pts to 14 pts in half-point increments, to satin aluminium shim with 6 pts, 12 pts, millimetres and inches. (Fig **2.3**)

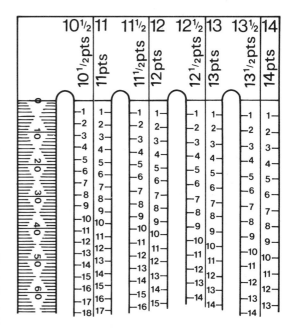

2.3 *A typical depth scale. This is of white plastic with a total of 16 point sizes, plus inches and millimetres. It is able to measure a depth of 300 mm (or an A4 page)*

2.34 Whatever the material or combination of scales they will include a scale of 12 pts (which equals picas or ems) so that the depth scale can also be used for horizontal and vertical measurement of pictures or spaces.

TYPE SCALES

2.35 Usually of stainless steel in a variety of graduations, one of the commonest being 8, 10 and 12 pts with either inches or millimetres on the fourth edge. (Fig **2.4**)

2.36 A useful form is the conversion type scale where the point size is related to a millimetre scale so that measurements may be read off directly in ems or millimetres. (Fig **2.5**) A further development is the use of chrome steel which has a matt surface.

REPRODUCTION COMPUTER

2.37 This is a useful aid for ascertaining the reproduction size of original art work together with the percentage of enlargement or reduction.

2.38 It consists of two discs pivoted at their centres and graduated at the outer edges. The present dimensions of the art work are set one above the other on the scales, and the new ones read off in the same relative positions – to the left for reductions and the right for enlargements. (Fig **2.6**) For percentage enlargement or reduction, the present size is set under the new size on the scales when the percentage will appear in a cut-out window.

2.39 It is particularly useful where a drawing has to fit a given space or where the designer needs to know the finished size of art work in order to lay out a page. The photographer will use it for computing the percentage adjustment necessary for setting up his camera.

LIGHTBOX

2.40 This unit can be obtained in a separate, portable form for desk top operation or combined with a stand giving adjustable height and angle. (Fig **2.7**)

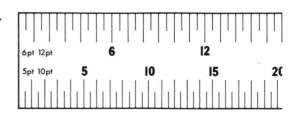

2.4 *A typical stainless steel type scale with a length of 300 mm*

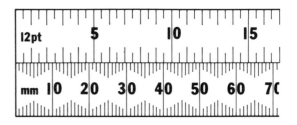

2.5 *A conversion type scale with which measurements in millimetres may be read off in ems, and vice versa*

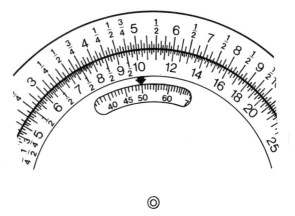

2.6 *A reproduction computer. The setting shows a picture 5″ × 10″. If the 5″ dimension were reduced to 3″ or enlarged to 8″, it can be seen that the other dimension would be 6″ or 16″ respectively and that 5″ to 10″ equals the 50% increase as shown in the window*

2.41 The light source consists of two or more cold cathode tubes beneath an opalescent glass or plastic surface to give an even, diffused light without excessive heat. The better units have in addition a dimmer control.

2.42 The unit enables tracing to be more easily carried out and, if necessary, onto material which itself is not particularly translucent. It is also useful for sizing and marking up photographs, retouching film intermediates and overlay drafting.

PROJECTOR/VISUALISER

2.43 Though somewhat large in size, this is a relatively simple piece of equipment which works on the same principle as the photo-enlarger. (Fig **2.8**)

2.44 It has a copy-board at low level and a viewing surface of plate glass at a higher level. Between them is the lighting bowl and lens carrier. The copy-board and lens can be raised and lowered independently to focus the image of a picture on the copy-board onto the viewing surface. This image can be enlarged or reduced as required for appreciation of pictures or art work at their final size, or for tracing to form a new draft or original drawing to avoid tedious re-plotting.

2.45 Some units have the facility to print the image as a bromide which saves even the comparatively short time needed to trace direct from the viewing surface.

2.46 However simple the mechanics, such a machine is likely to be outside the means of most, but if access to such equipment can be obtained a lot of art work preparation can be made very much simpler.

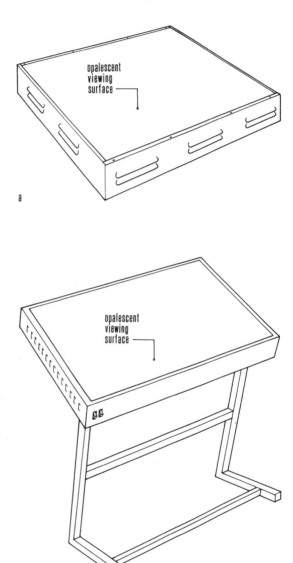

2.7 *Lightboxes for back illumination of art work or photographs.* (a) *Portable type for bench or desk top use,* (b) *Stand mounted to give adjustable height and angle*

Aids

2.47 Under this category comes a large range of miscellaneous items which are designed to save time and make repetitive work easier.

2.48 There is no shame in using a template to draw a circle instead of spring bows or compasses, always provided that the end result is satisfactory. The important thing is a good final product and if this is accomplished by the use of more graphic aids than less, then so be it. The illustrator is judged by the end result, not the means chosen to achieve it.

2.49 Do not, however, be obsessed about the use of aids. They are not all as successful as their publicity would have us believe. Use them when it is beneficial to do so, but if the circumstances warrant it do not hesitate to employ more traditional methods.

ERASERS

2.50 Erasure is an art in itself and is an important part of the drawing process whether it is for subsequent alteration, addition or just the removal of unwanted parts.

2.51 The eraser (commonly called an ink or pencil rubber) is familiar to everyone but with the introduction of new materials and media to match, a new generation of erasers has evolved.

2.52 It is not proposed to list all the variants and their particular attributes, for selection is, by and large, a matter of personal choice. There are however two basic rules to bear in mind when deciding which eraser to use.
(1) Use the softest possible compatible with the job in hand to avoid damage to the drawing surface.
(2) Use the eraser particularly designed for use on the material being drawn upon.

2.53 An example of the latter rule would be the use of the vinyl eraser which contains a chemical solvent. This will remove ink from polyester film as if by magic, but on tracing paper will leave a shadow image.

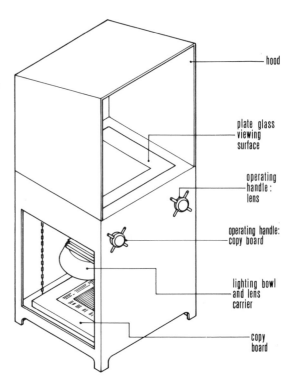

2.8 *Sketch of projector/visualiser showing the main component parts*

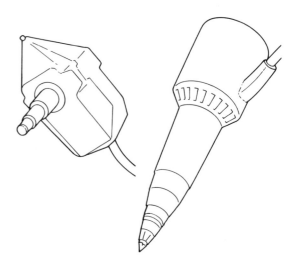

2.9 *Typical hand-held erasing machines. They can be obtained operated by mains electricity or rechargeable batteries*

2.54 Electric erasing machine This is used to advantage where larger areas need treatment. (Fig **2.9**) Care must be taken so that the softer surfaces of linen, drawing paper and some boards are not damaged by excessive pressure on the machine when in use. This could cause the depositing of heated rubber residue and the distortion of the sheet.

2.55 Erasing shield This should be used to protect the drawing surface and those parts of the drawing which do not need treatment. Choose a form with squared corners which will be found to be more versatile, enabling precise areas to be treated. (Fig **2.10**)

2.55 Erasing shield This should be used to tools for cleaning up and removing those small blemishes that the larger erasers cannot easily reach. The best blade for the job is the double-edged safety type (not the single edged, which is not flexible enough for this use).

2.57 For best results, the blade should be broken to provide a sharp point for fine work and a 'blunt' edge for general use. (Fig **2.11**) The advent of stainless steel has made the forming of these edges less easy as the blades bend rather than snap, and have to be cut. Scissors will do this quite well but leave a burr on one edge which needs smoothing off to avoid scratching the drawing surface.

2.58 The blade should be held between thumb and the first two fingers, keeping the edge parallel to the surface of the paper. (Fig **2.12**) Do not attempt to erase too quickly by heavy pressure or increasing the angle of the blade to paper surface, and use it only on materials which have hard, non-absorbent surfaces such as tracing paper and polyester film. The surface of materials with a softer surface will need to be burnished after erasure if ink is to be used, otherwise the lines will appear ragged.

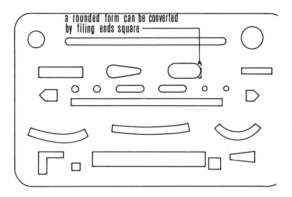

2.10 *Erasing shields are available in many patterns. Those with squared apertures are best, but if they are not readily obtainable it is possible to file down rounded edges*

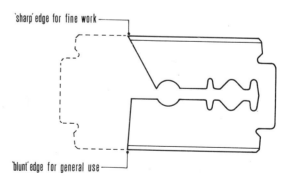

2.11 *Where the razor blade should be broken to provide the necessary working edges*

MASKING AGENTS

2.59 On a par with erasers are the aids which conceal blemishes and those parts of illustrations which are not required, rather than remove them. They are useful where the unwanted parts cannot be permanently obscured or where the material surface is unsuitable for erasure.

2.60 Process white This, or any of the white correction fluids, is invaluable for retouching where the marks of previous erasure are still visible or for spotting out small blots or blemishes.

2.61 Process black This is equally useful for touching in black areas and, being of a thicker consistency than the normal waterproof inks, it will not distort the thinner, less stable materials and is easier to control.

2.62 Photo-opaque film Where large areas of black are required it is easier and quicker to use one of the light-fast materials instead of painting out. These are obtainable in dry transfer sheets about 650 × 500 mm or in rolls, 800 mm × 25 m. They consist of a clear acetate backing with the light-fast (or photo-opaque) film lightly bonded to the face. This film is coloured ruby red or amber, and the art work can be seen beneath it so that accurate cutting and alignment can be carried out.

2.63 The coloured film is cut and peeled away from the acetate except for those areas that are required to be black. The same method and material are used to prepare tint overlays (*see* section 6, on tints and screens).

2.64 Cellulose tape This is 10 to 15 mm wide and of the same light-fast colour. It is used to define the perimeters of photographs, art work or film intermediates without having to erase or cut away the unwanted areas. Be careful to use this tape only on materials with hard surfaces as removal after use will damage the softer, more absorbent materials.

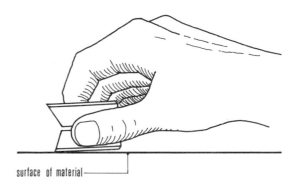

2.12 *How the blade should be held. It is important to keep the edge near parallel to the drawing surface. The action should be a steady sweep across the work rather than digging into the material surface*

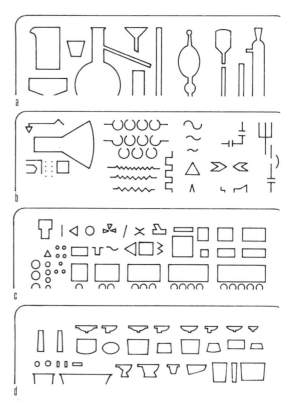

2.13 *Some of the templates for specialist use by 'Linex'.* (a) *Plumbing* (b) *Ventilating* (c) *Electronics* (d) *Chemistry*

TEMPLATES

2.65 These is an ever increasing range of aids covering geometrical shapes of all sizes and a variety of symbols likely to be needed in architecture and engineering, the specialist disciplines of heating, ventilating and electronics, to work study and computer programming. (Fig **2.13**)

2.66 They are invariably of transparent plastic in green, blue or orange. Some have a bevelled edge so that by reversing the template they can be used for pen or pencil while others have 'pips' or bosses on one side to provide the same facility.

2.67 Choose templates with care for they are not cheap, and because there are many variations of a similar shape, hasty selection can result in a surfeit of little used, expensive items.

DRY TRANSFER

2.68 Almost matching the range offered by solid templates are those available in dry transfer form. Lettering, symbols, tints and screens are dealt with in other chapters, but there are still many forms of arrows, solid and broken rules, square and rounded corners to suit the rules, brackets, circles, etc. (Fig **2.14**)

2.69 As with templates, use these sheets selectively, ensuring that the end result will justify their use. While they are certainly useful, it should be recognised that they do have limitations and are not necessarily the answer to every illustrator's prayer.

2.70 Finally, most of the equipment manufacturers have a supporting range of graphic art products such as line tapes, spray adhesives and protective coatings, swivel-head knives, burnshers, self-sealing cutting mats, etc., which, though too numerous to detail here, will at some time or another be found useful.

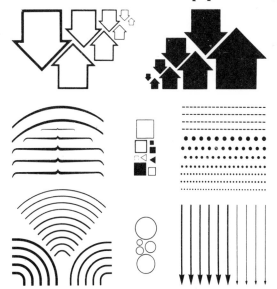

2.14 *A selection of the dry transfer forms which may be used to advantage in selected circumstances*

3 Enlargement and Reduction

Introduction

3.1 Most of the art work for reproduction is likely to be subjected to enlargement or reduction techniques at some stage or another. This is not to say that the final set of illustrations will always consist of a mixture of the two but, as will be seen later, both have a part to play in the production process.

3.2 It is important to determine at an early stage the extent to which these techniques will be applied to the particular job on which you are working, as other factors, e.g. line thickness and spacing, lettering size, etc., will depend upon that decision.

3.3 Drawing materials are much coarser than the materials used for photography and the instruments and media currently available together impose limitations on the quality of hand-drawn art work. Generally, therefore, enlargement should be restricted to camera based 'mechanical' art work such as photo-setting, dry transfer lettering and symbols, line and half-tone pictures, etc., while reduction can be applied to all art work, whether camera or hand produced.

Enlargement

3.4 When speaking of enlargement it is easy to imagine a snap shot increased to portrait size without a visible loss of definition. With such a picture, viewed at a distance of a few feet, the enlargement is not displeasing. To apply the same principle to line art work, however, is to court disaster, for it is not possible to produce hand-drawn art work which can be successfully enlarged.

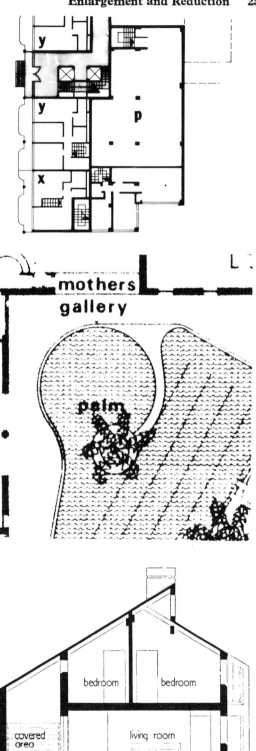

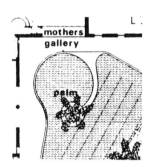

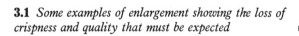

3.1 *Some examples of enlargement showing the loss of crispness and quality that must be expected*

3.5 However good the initial drawing may be, its quality cannot be improved upon by any form of enlargement. Lines and lettering lose their sharpness, edges become furry, any slight imperfections will be exaggerated and overall will do nothing to enhance the illustrator's reputation. (Fig **3.1**) Preparing art work for enlargement should whenever possible be avoided and, from an aesthetic point of view, vigorously opposed should it be suggested.

3.6 Enlargement does, of course, have its uses and an important one concerns the preparation of draft material or author's copy for redrawing. It will often be found that these drafts are a motley collection made up of different styles, sizes and scales gathered together from many sources.

3.7 It is at this draft stage that decisions have to be made regarding the amount of detail required to be shown, how large or small the illustration is to be in its final form and following from there what reduction should be applied.

3.8 It is very difficult to assess these points when the basic material varies so much, and it is here that the enlargement of some of the drafts to bring them up to the size and scale of the others will save much time and make the final art work much easier to prepare. (Fig **3.2**)

3.9 Such enlargement is easy to achieve by photographic means, and the resulting bromide print is then used as the draft in place of the author's copy. Whilst on the subject of bromide prints, it may also be noted that over-sized material can be subjected equally well to photographic adjustment to make all the drafts as far as possible consistent in size and scale.

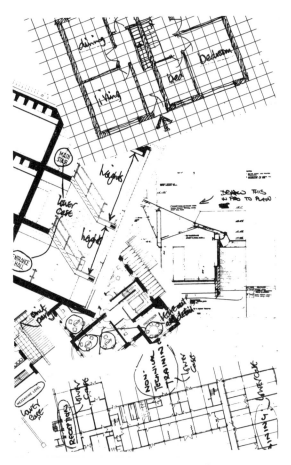

3.2 *Drafts of different sizes and scales are difficult to relate and should whenever possible be brought to the same proportions to make production easier*

Reduction

3.10 There is no arguing the fact that any art work, no matter what the subject, can gain in quality and appearance when some degree of reduction is applied – always provided that the art work has been prepared with such reduction in mind. Lines and lettering become sharper and denser and those small blemishes tend to disappear. (Fig. **3.4,** pages 28 and 29)

3.11 In order to take full advantage of the benefits that reduction of art work can offer, there are several points that need to be considered before putting pencil to paper.

3.12 First, when a drawing is subjected to a normal reduction, both vertical and horizontal dimensions are diminished so that while their area becomes smaller, the proportion remains the same. It is important to realise that when one speaks of a 2:1 reduction, the result is not *half* the original area but a *quarter*, and similarly a 3:1 reduction will be $\frac{1}{9}$ of the original; 4:1 equals $\frac{1}{16}$ and so on. (Fig. **3.3**)

3.13 It will be evident from this that art work to be prepared for a 6:1 reduction, for example, will need very careful thought regarding line thickness, spacing, letter size and amount of detail to be shown.

3.14 Second, it follows that the original material must be critically assessed in order to ensure that the essential information will be visible when the proposed reduction has been applied. Ideally, then, all the drafts should be assembled together so that it can be seen that the reduction factor will be suitable for all the illustrations and not just for some.

3.15 It is quite possible that all the draft material will not be available at the same time but given out in chapters or other groupings. In such a case, a decision will have to be made based on the material to hand and then it should be ensured if possible that the remaining copy is produced in the same form and size.

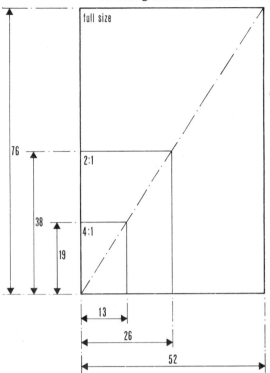

3.3 *How reduction affects the area but not the proportion of a diagram*

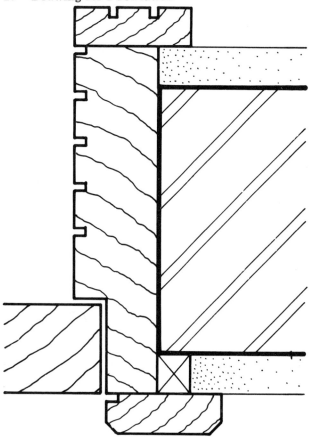

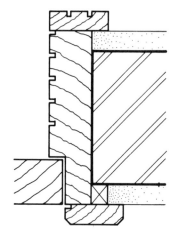

3.4 *Some examples of reduction compared with the original artwork*

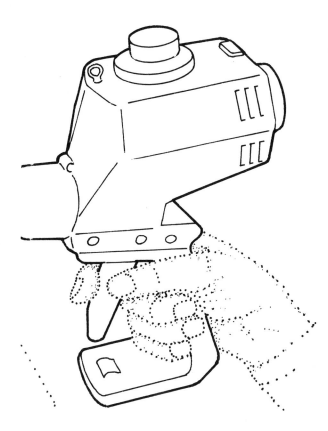

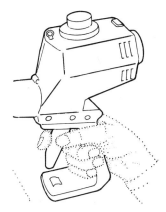

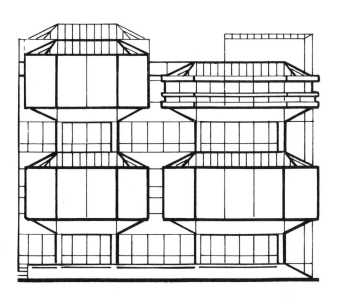

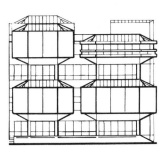

3.16 In any event, try to secure as much as possible in the first instance so that a consistent style can be decided upon at an early stage. This is also the point at which the copy can be adjusted in size, by photographic means or where the form is relatively simple, by proportional dividers, pantograph or projector.

3.17 Third, the aim should be to use the same reduction throughout the set of illustrations. Using the same reduction means that all the line weights, lettering, shading patterns or tints will be consistent, making the drawing process that much easier and requiring fewer materials.

3.18 The photographer will also benefit, for having set up his camera for the first diagram he has no further adjustment to make to shoot the rest of the set.

3.19 Fourth, having decided upon the reduction and prepared the art work accordingly, do not allow it to be changed arbitrarily to suit last minute adjustments of the page design. It sometimes happens at the layout stage that there is not enough, or too much, text to fit on a page and rather than get copy altered and reset it would be quicker (and cheaper) to get a drawing or two remade smaller or larger to fit the new space.

3.20 However convenient this may be, it should be resisted because:
(1) There is no point in making necessarily detailed preparations to achieve consistency if it is to be summarily changed at the last moment.
(2) Any difference in size, density or scale between illustrations will be easily discernible when viewed collectively, upsetting the balance and spoiling the continuity of the set. (Fig **3.5**)
(3) No designer would surely subscribe to the principle of increasing or decreasing the point size of a block of text in order for it to fit a larger or smaller space, and there is no valid reason why the art work and text (which are to be read together) should be treated differently.

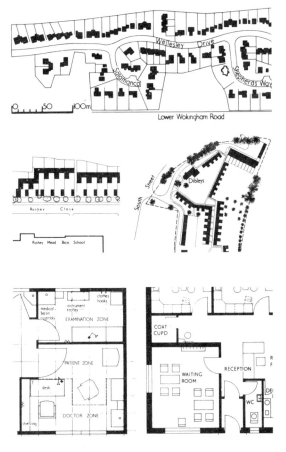

3.5 *The discernible difference apparent when art work drawn for the same reduction is in fact altered in size*

3.21 It is understandable that the designer will not want to delay the work unnecessarily at the layout stage, but any drawing that is required to fit a different sized space should be redrawn to fit that space and not merely adjusted photographically.

3.22 Finally, while a reduction will generally enhance a drawing, do not use it to excess. A drawing for a 12:1 reduction, for example, will need a very large sheet on which to prepare the art work. It will take longer to draw and be thus more expensive. It will need at least two – probably four – separate camera shots, as most copyboards will not take a very large sheet. (In general it is a good idea if possible to find out the camera copyboard size. The maximum size of the prepared art work should preferably not exceed this.) Combinations of negatives prior to the final camera shot, plus the loss of quality at each stage, plus the additional production costs will largely negate any advantage that may have been envisaged.

Marking Up

3.23 Whether the intention is to enlarge, reduce or reproduce same-size, the art work requires to be marked up, i.e. some indication must be made of the treatment the art work is to receive, and one or two points should be considered in order to make the production process as clear and straightforward as possible.

3.24 Remember that the photographer is not a mind reader. He will be seeing the art work for the first time and has no idea how each of the diagrams is intended to be read. General instructions and those for any special treatments must therefore be written legibly and unambiguously to avoid any misunderstanding. (Fig. **3.6**)

3.25 Indication of enlargement or reduction must likewise be capable of easy recognition and understanding. Even if this works out as an exact ratio, e.g. 2:1, 3:1, 5:1, etc., it is always preferable to draw a horizontal line corresponding to the overall width of the drawing which the photographer can measure to check that he

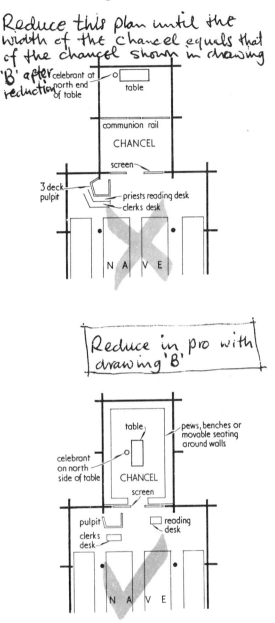

3.6 *Keep the instructions simple and legible*

has applied the correct adjustment of size. This line should be positioned well clear of any part of the drawing to avoid any subsequent complicated spotting out after photography. (Fig **3.7**)

3.26 When indicating the new size on any art work make sure that the units are clearly shown and preferably in millimetres or pica points (or ems). The photographer will probably convert the difference in size into a percentage up or down to set up his camera, but whatever he does he must be able to read the dimensions specified. (Fig **3.8**)

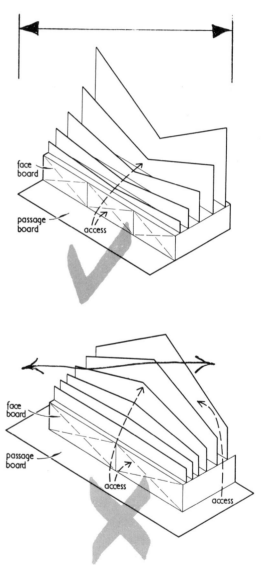

3.7 *A line that can be easily measured is best to show the required size of an illustration. Keep it away from any part of the drawing so that it can be clearly seen and will not need to be spotted out after photography*

Same-size

3.27 Dwelling briefly on the third method of reproduction, i.e. one-to-one or same-size, it is difficult to make such a strong case against it as against enlargement, especially if the standard of draughtsmanship is high.

3.28 It is certainly a fact that it will not improve on reproduction, and for every process between original art work and final printing, some loss of quality must be expected. The final result could be satisfactory or less so depending more upon the skill and patience of the photographer and printer than that of the illustrator.

3.29 If the art work is not mixed with any that has been given different treatment, i.e. enlarged or reduced, then the final result could be success-ful. Lettering, however, could be a problem if it is to be applied by the illustrator. In order not to appear too large it would have to be around 8 or 10 pts, i.e. about 2 or 3 mm high, which is small by anyone's standards and must not, therefore, be expected to be easily applied.

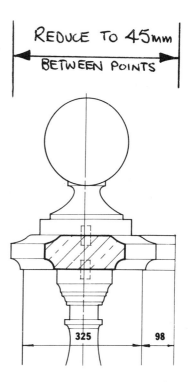

3.8 *The units used to indicate the new size must be clearly shown and familiar to the photographer*

Introduction

4.1 It is not intended here to direct the reader through all the mechanics of line drawing nor to dictate what types of line to use for this or that situation. These decisions are the same whether drawing for reduction or not and whatever the purpose of the illustration.

4.2 When drawing for same-size reproduction, what can be seen by the naked eye can in general terms be reproduced. A xerox, diazo or ozalid process will faithfully copy what has been drawn whether in ink, pencil or other medium however quickly or roughly the original was prepared.

4.3 For reduction purposes however, some discipline has to be introduced and thought given to such things as line quality, thickness and spacing. From these, other factors evolve, such as addition of detail, shape and form, but basically it is the line that requires the most attention.

Quality of Lines

4.4 The line is the basis of most illustrations and while pencil and ink are the most commonly used media, it is the ink line which is of paramount importance when drawing for the camera.

4.5 The line must be photo-opaque, i.e. black and dense to prevent the passage of light and give a good contrast with the base material. (Fig **4.1**) It must be sharp and clear and the correct weight for the type and style of the drawing. Above all, it must be of the right thickness to suit the reduction which is to be applied.

4.1 *The lines on the left are good examples of photo-opaque lines. Those on the right are the same thickness but of poorer quality because they are less dense*

4.6 Especially where translucent materials are used, all linework should be drawn on the face which is to be exposed to the camera. Do not try to achieve textural or tonal difference by part drawing on the back of the sheet. This will show grey and will cause problems with photography especially if the base material is thick. (Fig **4.2**)

4.2 *The lines on the left were drawn on the* face *of smooth-surfaced tracing paper. Compare with those on the right which were drawn on the* reverse

Thickness of Lines

4.7 With ink line drawings any change of emphasis or expression, of shape or spatial distance must rely on the variation of thickness and spacing of lines (as distinct from textural or tonal value which is achieved by the addition of tints and screens as described in section 6).

4.8 Considering line thickness, the establishment of a hierarchy is important to achieve form and expression and need not consist of more than three weights, bold or primary, medium or secondary and fine. (Fig **4.3**)

4.3 *A typical hierarchy of lines drawn for a 2:1 reduction. Shown, left, as drawn and, right, after reduction*

4.9 The thickness of each weight is largely a personal decision influenced by the style of the illustrator, to an extent the type of illustration and the requirements of the author, but, most of all, the reduction to be applied to those lines.

4.10 It is true to say that if the finest (or thinnest) line drawn can be reproduced, then all the others in the hierarchy can likewise be reproduced. It follows then that the first step must be to determine the fine line thickness.

4.11 There are only two factors to consider. First, what the *published* fine line thickness will be and, second, what reduction will be applied to the art work.

4.12 The line thickness will to an extent be governed by the quality of paper being used for printing, but for all normal purposes can be specified as 0·1 mm. It is possible to go as fine as 0·05 mm, but this will need very high quality preparation and materials and may well be unnecessarily demanding.

4.13 The reduction will have been decided upon during the assessment of the draft material, and if you are fortunate this may be constant throughout the set. But, as is often the case, you may have to deal with two or more, and it is important to indicate clearly on each draft the reduction for which it is to be drawn. Do not rely on your memory, it may well be a week or more before you see some of the material again.

4.14 These two factors then being known, the fine line thickness to be drawn is found by simply multiplying the published thickness decided upon by the reduction factor or ratio. For example, with a published fine line thickness of 0·1 mm, an illustration to be drawn for a 3:1 reduction will have fine lines drawn to a thickness of 0·3 mm; for a 4:1 reduction they will be 0·4 mm, and so on. From this fine line thickness the medium and bold lines of the hierarchy can be established.

4.15 As mentioned before, the differentiation within the hierarchy is a matter of personal choice but remember that it must be discernible. If graphic definition of form is to be expressed by contrast in line thickness, such contrast must be able to be seen, and seen easily. (Fig **4.4**)

4.16 An indication of suitable line thicknesses for various reductions can be seen in the table. (Fig **4.5**) This has been found to work satisfactorily and can be used as a guide. Bear in mind though, that the values represent the ideal in terms of line quality and base material.

4.17 Do not, therefore, expect a 0·2 mm line to give a good result if it does not conform to the standard or if it is drawn on anything other than a smooth, hard surface.

4.4 *The differentiation between lines of a hierarchy must be clearly visible. Compare the poor contrast on the left with that shown on the right*

reduction	line thickness in mm		
	fine	medium	bold
2 : 1	0·2	0·4	0·8
3 : 1	0·3	0·5	1·0
4 : 1	0·4	0·6	1·2
5 : 1	0·5	0·8	1·5
6 : 1	0·6	1·0	1·8
7 : 1	0·7	1·0	2·1
8 : 1	0·8	1·2	2·4
10 : 1	1·0	1·5	3·0
12 : 1	1·2	1·8	3·6

4.5 *The table shows line thicknesses suitable for various reductions which will reproduce satisfactorily under ideal conditions. Remember to make allowance for materials with less than a smooth, fine surface or media giving a poorer quality line*

4.18 If in doubt when choosing between two line thicknesses, incline to the bolder size. It is preferable to see a line clearly from beginning to end rather than one which breaks up or fades within its length. Similarly, where reductions fall between those stated, e.g. 3½:1, 5½:1 etc., they should be treated as the next higher ratio – unless of course, the technical pen range in use includes that particular size or sizes.

Spacing of Lines

4.19 The spacing of adjacent lines is governed principally by their thickness and the reduction to be used. Just as it is important to establish a hierarchy of lines, so it is important to position such lines so that they do not upset this balance by closing up on reduction, making them appear thicker than as drawn. (Fig **4.6**)

4.20 The majority of instances will occur when adding detail in the form of graphic symbols and other representation where lines are parallel and equidistant, such as staircases, brick courses, bolt threads, etc. In most cases the scale of the drawing will dictate the spacing, but if it should become too close for the reduction being used, then it must either be simplified or omitted altogether. (Fig **4.7**)

4.21 In the case of expression of shape or form where the line spacing is required to diminish – to show a curved surface for instance – then more care is necessary to prevent the closing up of these lines. In general these lines should be fine rather than medium or bold, and of constant thickness. Start always at the 'darkest' edge, i.e. where the spacing is closest, and work back to the 'lightest', wider spacing. (Fig **4.8**)

4.22 Finally, remember (a) that the larger the reduction, the wider should be the spacing and (b) never draw bold lines with less than their own thickness separating them. (Fig **4.9**)

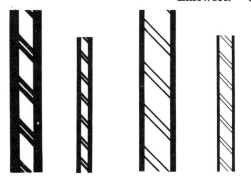

4.6 *Adjacent lines must be spaced according to line thickness and reduction. Compare those on the left – before and after reduction – with those on the right*

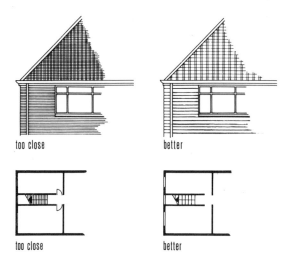

too close   better

too close   better

4.7 *With drawings of small scale or for large reductions the line spacing must be drawn 'out of scale' or omitted to avoid the lines closing up*

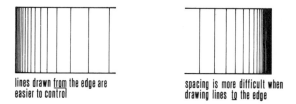

lines drawn <u>from</u> the edge are easier to control

spacing is more difficult when drawing lines <u>to</u> the edge

4.8 *More care than usual must be taken when drawing lines where the spacing diminishes to show form. It is also much easier to draw such lines from 'dark' to 'light', i.e. start from the edges and work inwards*

Construction Lines

4.23 It is seldom possible to finalise an illustration without at least drafting it out in skeleton form, and the usual medium for this is the pencil.

4.24 The method of finalising this pencil draft will depend on the style of the illustrator but the quickest method is undoubtedly to ink over the pencil lines and then erase the superfluous construction work to leave a clean and tidy illustration.

4.25 To save even more time it should not be necessary to erase these extra construction lines if they are light and grey rather than dense and black.

4.26 Under the lamps of the camera copyboard light, grey pencil lines will not compete with dense black ink and will disappear, especially if a reduction is involved (Fig **4.10**), but remember that if this technique is employed, *the lines must be light and must be grey.*

4.27 The choice of pencil grade will depend upon the 'tooth' of the material used and therefore no rigid rules can be applied, but in general the aim should be to use the hardest grade the material will take, compatible with visibility. Too soft a grade will tend to make the construction line blacker and thus more likely to reproduce and, worse, will deposit loose graphite on the surface which will make the art work dirty.

Blue Lines

4.28 Blue pencils are traditionally used for setting out and positioning diagrams, guidelines for ranging blocks of lettering or notes and any instruction or labelling necessary for the reproduction of the art work but which is not itself required to be reproduced.

4.29 Normally, anything drawn or lettered in blue is invisible under the camera lighting and should not reproduce. In practical terms, however, this is very much subject to the density of the line and the shade of blue used.

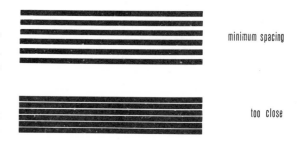

minimum spacing

too close

4.9 *Bold lines should have at least their own width separating them, otherwise they will close up on reduction. When several bold lines join together, the result can be startling*

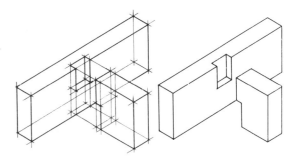

4.10 *Both drawings used pencil construction lines but the left-hand one was drawn with an HB, while the other used a 4H*

4.30 A sky or an ultramarine blue will be found to be satisfactory but a darker shade such as indigo, especially if used with heavy pressure, will quite likely produce an image – perhaps only a ghost line, but nevertheless visible. (Fig **4.11**)

4.31 Be at least as careful with blue lines as with pencil construction lines. Keep them as light as possible for they are not easy to erase because of the colour pigment, and the type of eraser needed to remove them could just as well damage the ink work.

Drawing Technique

4.32 With all pure-line drawings the information to be conveyed and the character of the illustration depends to a great extent on the variable line weights used and the degree of discernible difference between them.

4.33 A comparatively simple but effective technique employing these principles involves the selection of features of orthographic elevations which can be given more definition. These include windows, doors, projecting elements such as eaves, etc. which are enclosed on one or two sides by a bolder line corresponding to a shadow. (Fig **4.12**)

4.34 For three-dimensional illustrations the same bolder line given to profile or silhouette lines (as distinct from lines indicating internal changes of plane) will convey more information about the shape and depth of the subject being drawn. (Fig **4.13**)

4.35 Whatever the technique employed, be careful to relate the treatment to the type of illustration. An engineering subject designed to be read by engineers should conform to the disciplined conventions normally applied to such illustrations, while an architect will more readily follow drawings executed in a style familiar to him.

4.11 The effect of using a dark blue pencil. In the box on the right were written the instructions to the photographer – but in light blue

4.12 An example of an elevation using the bold line technique

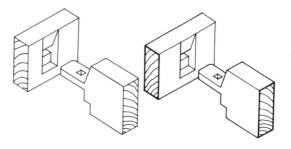

4.13 This shows two similar isometric drawings with no treatment on the left-hand example, compared with the bold line technique given to the right-hand drawing

4.36 One cannot evolve a technique that can be adopted for all types of illustration even if this were remotely desirable. If guidance is required, this should be readily obtainable from the commissioning author, if not then his profession and that of the proposed readers should provide some useful pointers.

4.37 Whatever style is adopted, the aim of the illustrator should be to provide the photographer with as near perfect an illustration as possible in terms of quality of line, contrast and suitability for the proposed reduction. After the author, the most important critic to satisfy is the camera.

5 Graphic Symbols and Conventional Representation

Introduction

5.1 Symbols and conventions are used to avoid repetitive descriptions and notes (Fig **5.1**), to differentiate between materials (Fig **5.2**), to clarify shape (Fig **5.3**) and, to a somewhat lesser degree, indicate physical form and function. They are of particular importance in the sphere of publication where space and time are usually at a premium.

5.2 What constitutes the best symbol or convention for an element, be it a material, fixture, fitting or feature, is very much a matter of personal opinion, and the absence of adequate definitive standards in some areas tends towards the 'improvement' of some of the partially accepted recommendations. (Fig **5.4**)

5.3 As will be seen later in the chapter there is indeed room for individual variation (and, no doubt, improvement of some forms) but remember that any graphical representation should be used with discretion and have real purpose.

5.4 Whatever symbol or convention is used it must be considered as part of the illustration and as such must relate to it in terms of size, weight and, to a rather lesser degree, position.

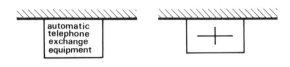

5.1 *How a standard symbol avoids the use of long descriptive notes*

5.2 *How conventional representation differentiates between materials*

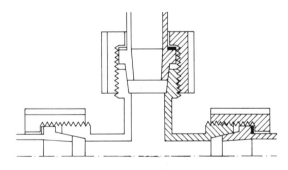

5.3 *How the use of a conventional line hatch can clarify the shape of an element*

5.4 *How some recommended symbols can be improved upon*

5.5 Regarding size, the symbol must obviously be discernible but not so large as to be out of scale with the illustration. (Fig **5.5**) Its weight or density should likewise balance, not being excessively darker than the drawing but not so light as to be lost on reproduction. (Fig **5.6**) Position is probably the least critical, certainly in respect of symbols depicting specialist equipment or conventions indicating materials, as their locations are mostly predetermined. If a key is necessary, however, care should be taken to ensure that it is positioned such that the illustration is not visually unbalanced.

Non-Variable Graphic Symbols

5.6 Symbols which are related to specialist disciplines, e.g. air-conditioning, electrical, fire protection, etc., cannot be too specific pictorially because of their size or complexity of detail and are therefore fairly schematic in form. (Fig **5.7**)

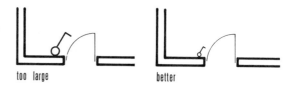

too large   better

5.5 *The size of the symbol or convention must not be out of scale with the illustration*

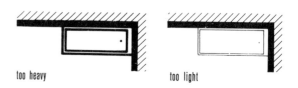

too heavy   too light

5.6 *The weight or density should be neither too dark nor too light*

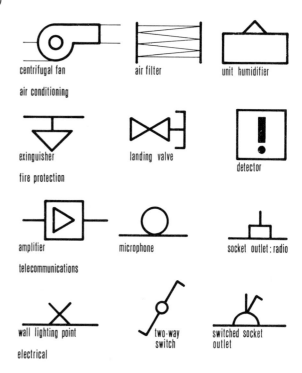

centrifugal fan   air filter   unit humidifier

air conditioning

exinguisher   landing valve

fire protection   detector

amplifier   microphone   socket outlet : radio

telecommunications

wall lighting point   two-way   switched socket
                       switch   outlet

electrical

5.7 *A selection from the range of symbols related to specialist disciplines. There are no specific recommendations regarding the size or scale of these symbols as they should relate to the scale of the illustration or the importance placed on the symbol itself*

5.7 When using these symbols it is important that the standard patterns are used without variation in order to ensure correct interpretation. (Fig **5.8**)

5.8 Many of the more regularly used symbols can be drawn using templates (Fig **5.9**) or applied from dry transfer sheets (Fig **5.11**), both generally available in two or more different scales. Because of the variety of manufacturers, however, and the preference towards their own national standards, care should be taken to ensure that the patterns used will conform to the author's or publisher's requirements. Additionally, ensure that the line weights of the template-drawn or applied-transfer symbols will match those of the illustration with which they are to be included. (Fig **5.10**)

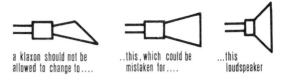

a klaxon should not be allowed to change to.... ..this, which could be mistaken for.... ...this loudspeaker

5.8 *Because specialist symbols are used to convey important information between members of the construction or design team, the standard pattern should not be varied in any way*

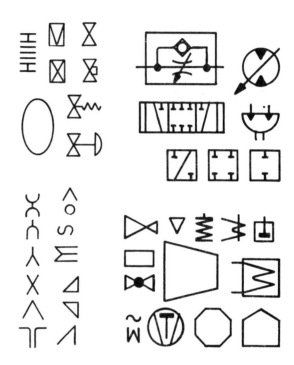

5.9 *Some typical template symbols. Remember to use a line weight that matches your diagram*

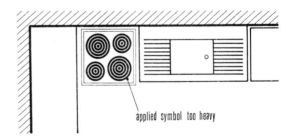

applied symbol too heavy

5.10 *Ensure that the line weights of the template-drawn or applied symbol will match those of the illustration*

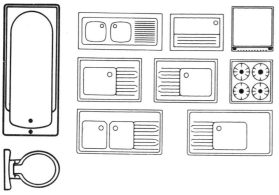

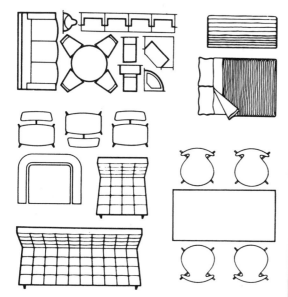

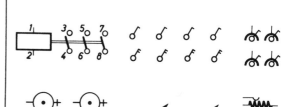

5.11 *A selection from the large range of dry transfer symbols currently available. Because of the variety of designs, be selective and choose those which will enhance your illustration*

Variable Graphic Symbols

5.9 Symbols which are not subject to the same discipline as those for the specialist contractors or consultants are those which present a more graphic picture of the element, e.g. stairs, trees, furniture, etc., which are in effect aerial views of the elements. (Fig **5.12**)

5.10 Here there is much more discretion in design and detail because (a) their nature and location make them easier to identify, (b) there is a lack at present of specific recommendation thus inviting individual design, and (c) we are used to seeing so many variations anyway, that almost any shape or pattern would be recognisable in its location.

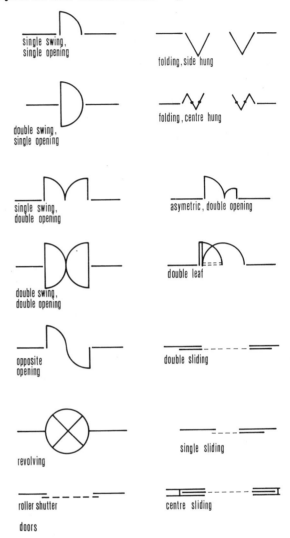

single swing, single opening

folding, side hung

double swing, single opening

folding, centre hung

single swing, double opening

asymetric, double opening

double swing, double opening

double leaf

opposite opening

double sliding

revolving

single sliding

roller shutter

centre sliding

doors

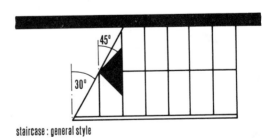

staircase : general style

5.12 *Some symbols which, because of their more pictorial presentation, can be varied to suit the individual illustrator's style* *(continued on page **46**)*

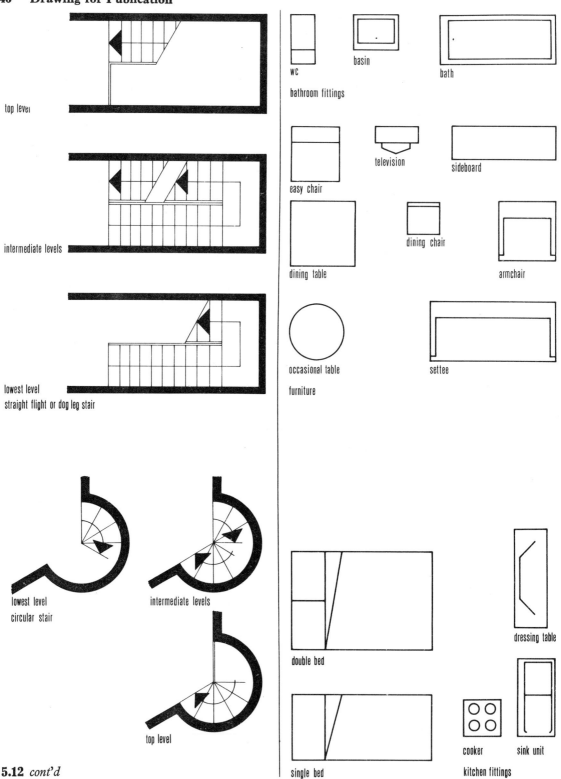

top level

intermediate levels

lowest level
straight flight or dog leg stair

lowest level
circular stair

intermediate levels

top level

5.12 *cont'd*

wc

basin

bath

bathroom fittings

easy chair

television

sideboard

dining table

dining chair

armchair

occasional table

settee

furniture

double bed

dressing table

single bed

cooker

sink unit

kitchen fittings

Conventional Representation

5.11 The representation of materials and features such as concrete, timber, embankments, etc., is another area where greater flexibility in design is to be found and for similar reasons to those described for symbols. (Fig **5.13**)

Variation of Symbols and Conventions

5.12 In all cases where there is latitude in the design and drawing of symbols and conventions, the illustrator must guard against over-enthusiasm which may result in their becoming too numerous, too complicated and, because there is a limit to discernible variation, too much alike in form or hatching. (Fig **5.14**)

5.13 *Forms of conventional representation covering building elements, materials, landscaping and external works* (*continued on page* **48**)

(*continued on page* **48**)

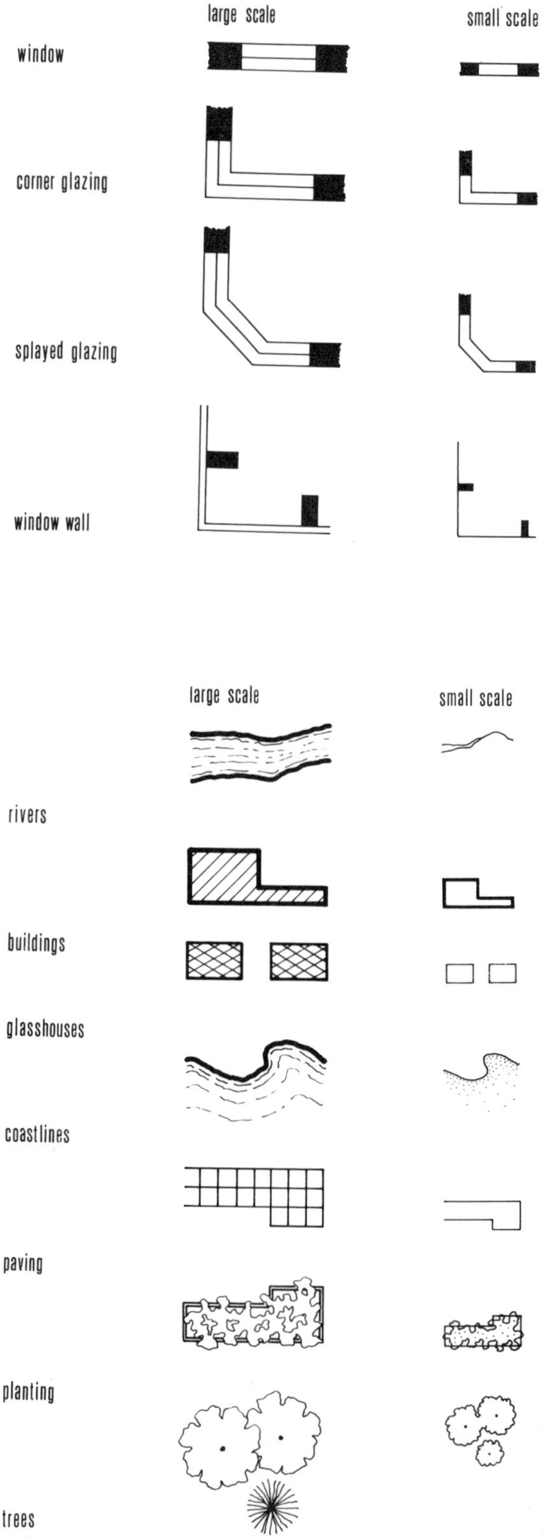

large scale

small scale

large scale

small scale

window

corner glazing

splayed glazing

window wall

embankment

cutting

railway

road

north point

5.13 (*above and left*)

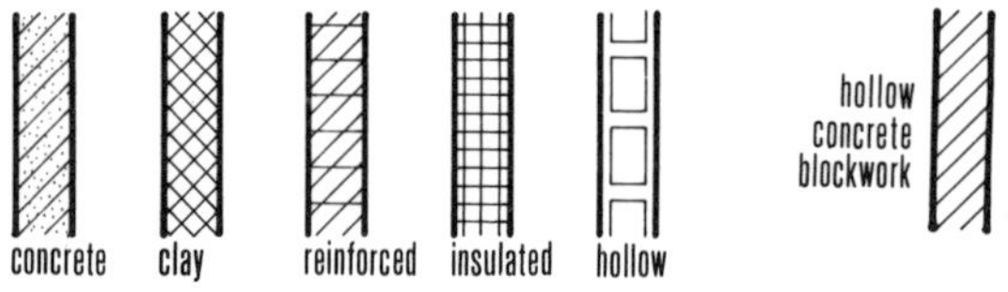

large scale

small scale

rivers

buildings

glasshouses

coastlines

paving

planting

trees

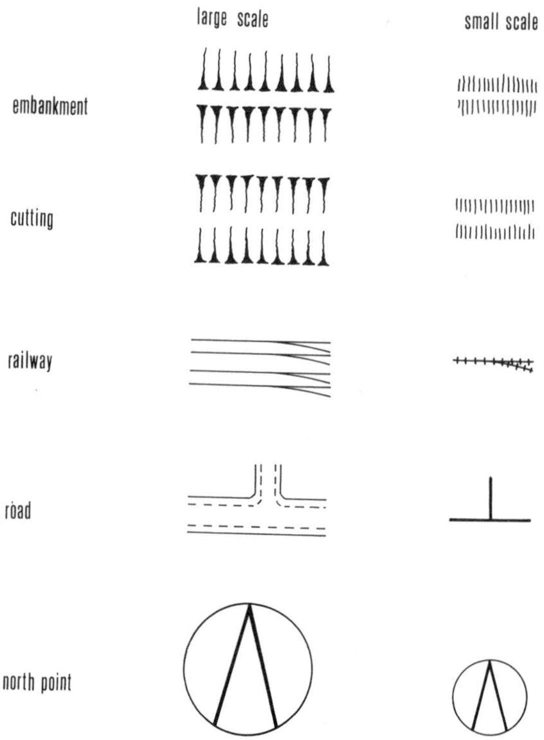

concrete   clay   reinforced   insulated   hollow

hollow
concrete
blockwork

5.14 *For most purposes the sub-division of an element into all its possible variations is unnecessary. In the example shown above, the standard blockwork convention with a note of the material would be sufficient*

5.13 To avoid these pitfalls, make sure your design conforms to the following simple guidelines:

(1) keep it clean and simple with no superfluous detail (Fig **5.15**)

(2) it should be easy to produce and thus quick to draw (Fig **5.16**)

(3) it must be distinctive, so that there can be no confusion with others (Fig **5.17**)

(4) it should be capable of being depicted in both large and small sized versions to allow for space and scale limitations (Fig **5.18**).

sink unit

5.15 *Keep the design simple with no superfluous detail*

chair

5.16 *It should be easy to draw*

tree

5.17 *It should be distinctive*

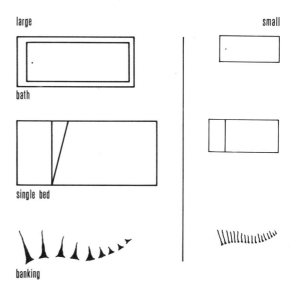

large   small

bath

single bed

banking

5.18 *It should be capable of being shown in large and small sized versions*

Additional Uses of Conventions

5.14 It is generally accepted that there is a need for graphic symbols. However, the argument for use of conventional representation remains fairly open, one side opting for its use exclusive of any accompanying notes and the other regarding any form of representation as superfluous.

5.15 Somewhere between the two is the technique of using conventions not to identify different materials, but to show interfaces and changes in plane. This can enhance the appearance of a drawing and usually takes the form of variations on line hatching (Fig **5.19**) but may also include dot tinting and other textural media. (Fig. **5.20**) Care must be taken when using this technique for it is easy to carry it to excess, leading to monotonous repetition. Do not, for example, attempt to cover all the surfaces, but restrict the treatment to emphasise only those parts where the materials differ or the planes change. (Fig **5.21**)

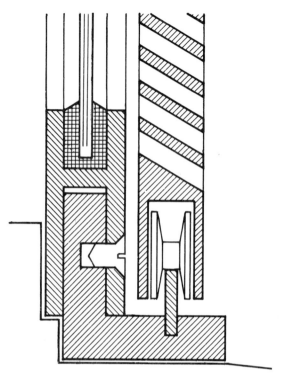

5.19 *The use of conventional line hatching to show interfaces*

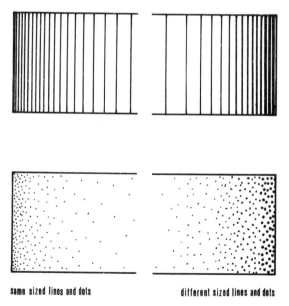

same sized lines and dots   different sized lines and dots

5.20 *Other methods of indicating form using lines and dots*

5.16 Additionally, because the hatching is not meant to indicate a particular material, keep the treatment simple, i.e. do not use too large a variation of textural patterns. (Fig **5.22**) The more repetitive the pattern used, the more obvious will be the intention (and the less the time needed to draw).

5.17 The use of patterns to identify development, landscaping and other areas in diagrammatic form also comes within this treatment category. Here the differences are shown by combinations of line and dot patterns which are usually accompanied by an identifying key.

5.18 Again, be careful not to use patterns that are too complex, particularly those which subdivide the area into very small segments which could close up on reproduction. (Fig **5.23**)

5.19 Avoid also those patterns which suggest a particular type of ground or feature which could mislead the reader, e.g. a pattern resembling a convention for water used to indicate a car parking area. (Fig **5.24**)

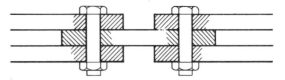

5.21 *Restriction of the treatment to critical areas saves time and can relieve the monotony of repetition*

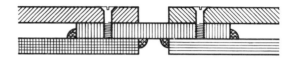

5.22 *Do not use too many different patterns or the emphasis will tend towards differing materials rather than interfaces*

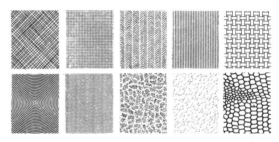

5.23 *Do not select complicated patterns which will not be suitable for reduction*

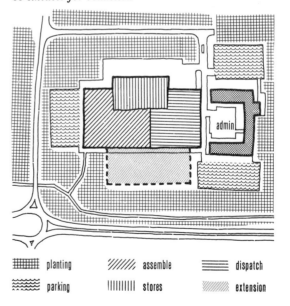

planting	assemble	dispatch
parking	stores	extension

5.24 *Avoid patterns which resemble a specific feature, unless they are to be used for that particular purpose*

5.20 Many of the dry transfer shading patterns currently available can be used successfully for this type of differentiation, but make sure that the weight and density will (a) match the illustration and (b) allow for any subsequent reduction. (Fig. **5.25**)

5.25 *Some of the range of dry transfer patterns which can be used in cartographical, geological and similar drawings.*

6 Tints and Screens

Introduction

6.1 To enable the illustrator to add tonal value or texture to a drawing, the use of shading patterns in the form of tints and screens has to be considered.

6.2 To avoid confusion between terms, a shading tint is defined as a ready-made pattern sheet which is applied to an illustration *before* photography. A screen tint is the grid of dots of varying gauges which is applied to a film intermediate *after* reduction.

6.3 It will be seen then that there are two methods by which differentiation can be achieved by mechanical means and further, that the illustrator can provide a third, that of hand drawing.

6.4 All three methods can be used separately or combined within the same set of illustrations, and though each has advantages and disadvantages, these are not necessarily common to them all.

6.5 So it will generally be found that if one method does not suit a particular requirement, one or both of the others will likely prove satisfactory. It is important therefore when considering tonal application to be flexible and relate each illustration to the method best suited to it.

Mechanical Methods

6.6 When using dot or line tints, whether applied before or after photography, it must first be determined which grades and densities will be most suitable. This is directly related to the quality of paper to be used; the better the paper, the finer the grade of tint and *vice versa*.

6.7 The grade and density of a dot tint is expressed in lines per inch (or centimetre) and a percentage (Fig **6.1**), and for line tints in lines per inch (or centimetre) coupled with a range of different line weights. (Fig **6.2**)

6.8 The printer will specify according to the paper quality at what grade (or screen) the half-tone pictures can be successfully reproduced and this must relate to the dot and line tints applied to the drawings.

6.9 It must be emphasised that the grade decided upon represents the maximum *after reduction*. For example, if 120 lines per inch is specified then for a 2:1 reduction, a maximum of 60 lines per inch should be used. For a 3:1 reduction, the maximum is 40 lines per inch and so on.

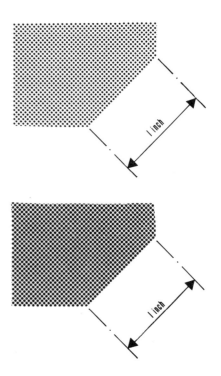

6.1 The grade of a dot tint expressed in simple terms equals the number of dots which can be accommodated in a distance of one inch (or one centimetre). The examples shown are both 30 lines per inch, but the upper one is 30% density while the lower one is 50%

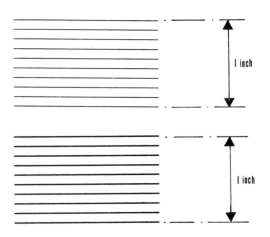

6.2 The grade of a line tint is also specified in lines per inch, but the density is ungraduated and depends upon random differences of line thickness. The examples are both 10 lines per inch

6.10 The density of a dot tint is specified as a percentage of solid black, so that 10% is very light while 70% is very dark. Most ranges have densities from 10 to 80% in increments of 10%, for each of the grades or screens in the series. (Fig **6.3**)

6.11 There is perhaps more flexibility with density than grade because the size of dot is less critical than the number, but nevertheless care should be exercised on two points.
(1) Do not subject tints at the extreme ends of a range to large reductions. A fine, light tint will not be discernible on reduction, while a fine, dark one will turn solid black. (Fig **6.4**) Experience will determine choice, but the table (Fig **6.5**) will be found useful as a general guide.
(2) When using tints in adjacent areas, remember to keep a difference of 20% in density between them. A good balance is maintained if the same grade or screen is used on the drawing but there will be better differentiation between 10% and 30% than, say, 10% and 20%. (Fig **6.6,** page 56)

6.3 *A typical sequence from a range of dot tints. The examples are all 30 lines per inch (or 11·75 lines per centimetre) and range from 10% density at the left to 80% at the extreme right in increments of 10%*

6.4 *Tints at the extreme ends of a range must be treated carefully or the desired effect can be frustrated. The example shows on the left, two tints at 50 lines per inch from opposite ends of the sequence. On the right are the same two tints having been subjected to a 2:1 reduction*

lines per inch	dot tints					
	light		medium		dark	
	10%	20%	30%	40%	50%	60%
27·5	2/3/4	2/3/4	2/3/4	2/3/4	2/3/4	2/3
30	2/3/4	2/3/4	2/3/4	2/3/4	2/3/4	2/3
32·5	2/3	2/3	2/3	2/3	2/3	•
42·5	2	2	2	2	•	•
50	2	2	2	2	•	•
55	2	2	2	2	•	•
60	2	2	2	2	•	•

⟵——————— range of reductions ———————⟶

6.5 *The table shows, for general guidance, the reductions to which various grades and densities of dot tints may be subjected under normal circumstances*

6.12 As stated earlier, there are two methods by which mechanical tints can be applied, and having dealt in general terms we must now look in more detail at how each method can be used to achieve its object.

Application to Art Work

6.13 In common with most graphic aids, the dry transfer has its limitations but it should be realised that these limitations vary according to the size of the drawing, the reduction to which it is to be subjected and the material on which the art work is drawn.

6.14 As a general rule, the larger the drawing the less use can be made of applied tonal media. This is simply because (a) the physical size of the areas to be treated may be larger than the dry transfer sheet and the invisible joining of two sheets is extremely difficult to achieve (Fig **6.7**) and (b) the range currently available, however comprehensive, does not cater for large reductions either in weight or the spacing of lines and dots.

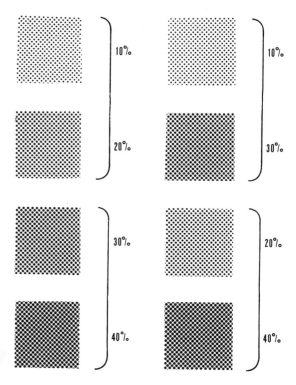

6.6 *Always try to maintain a difference in density of 20% between adjacent tints. There is a better contrast between the tints grouped as shown on the right than those shown left*

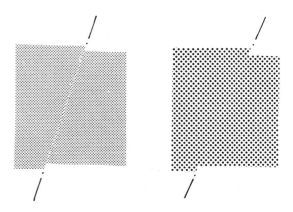

6.7 *Joining sections of dot tints is a difficult and tedious job if a satisfactory result is to be achieved. Almost impossible with a fine, light screen shown left, but easier with a coarse grade as shown right*

6.15 Additionally, large areas of flexible film should not be applied to another flexible surface, especially if the base material is not very stable. The adhesive is not strong enough to withstand a lot of handling and will allow movement between the film and the base material resulting in 'bubbles' and subsequent loss of reproduction quality. (Fig **6.8**) Drawings requiring the application of mechanical tints should either be prepared on art board or attached to a rigid backing to avoid excessive flexing when being handled.

6.16 When deciding which parts of a drawing will be tinted, avoid very small and intricate shapes where possible. Complex cutting can quickly become tedious and will lead to oversimplification of the outline resulting in an untidy, ragged appearance.

6.17 Where it is just a case of differentiating one space from another, lay the tint on the area easiest to trim. (Fig **6.9**)

6.18 Avoid laying the tints over the enclosing border lines and trimming to the outside edge. Except in the case of a light tint within a fine line border, this method of laying will make the lines appear thicker and ragged – the result will be further exaggerated in cases where the dot is large and combined with a bold enclosing line. (Fig **6.10**) Avoid this by cutting the tint to fit within the inside edge of enclosing lines. (Fig **6.11**)

6.8 The effect of 'bubbles' caused by differential movement between base material and film tint or careless application resulting in the lifting of tint over trapped pockets of air

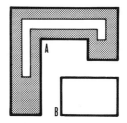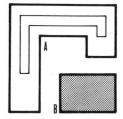

6.9 Where it does not matter whether A or B is tinted, choose the simpler shape. Do not make unnecessary work, you may well need that time at a later stage

6.10 Enclosing lines can look ragged when the tint is trimmed to the outside edge, particularly if the dot is large as shown

6.11 A much better effect is obtained if the tint is cut to just inside the inner edge of enclosing lines. The larger the reduction, the more space may be given

6.19 Be careful to select a pattern which is in scale with the parts being treated. It is defeating the object if the area to be tinted can only accommodate one dot of a screen or one line of a hatch, so choose a grade that will show enough of the pattern to be discernible. (Fig **6.12**)

6.20 When laying tints on translucent materials always apply them to the *face* of the drawing, *never* the reverse. Mechanical tints are printed on a carrier film with an adhesive layer, and however clear the film may be, there must be serious loss of definition when it is positioned on the back. The camera has in effect to penetrate the base material, plus the adhesive layer, plus the film in order to reach the *back* of the printed pattern, which in any case is never as black as the face. (Fig **6.13**)

6.21 Avoid, for the same reason, overlaying one tint upon another to effect a change of pattern. The loss of definition will be apparent even before photography and additionally could cause shadowing around the perimeter of the tinted area where the camera lighting cannot illuminate all the 'high' edges of the layers of tint. (Fig **6.14**)

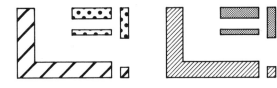

6.12 *Do not choose a pattern that is on too large a scale for the areas to be treated. Those shown on the left are of no use at all. You must relate the pattern to the smallest area to ensure correct differentiation, as shown on right*

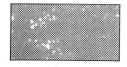 

6.13 *Always apply tints to the face of art work. The example shown on the left has the tint applied on the back. Compare the quality with the tint applied to the face, shown right*

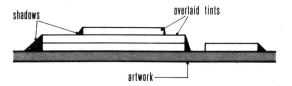

6.14 *Diagrammatic sketch showing the 'shadow' effect, which is difficult to overcome, when several tints are overlaid*

6.22 Remember also that the adhesive coating on sheets of tint will remove dry transfer lettering almost as efficiently as cellulose tape. Where such lettering has been applied, it must be protected by its silicone backing sheet to avoid accidental damage. (Fig **6.15**) It also helps if the tint is cut to size or nearly so before laying. Not only will this help to keep clear of any adjacent lettering but it is also a more economical use of the tint. (Fig **6.16**)

Application by Photographer

6.23 When a set of illustrations cannot be drawn for the same reduction or the areas to be tinted are very large, it may well be decided that the tints should be applied after the drawings have been reduced to their final size.

6.24 This will ensure that all the tints will match and conform exactly to the densities required but it is not, however, just a question of specifying the grade and density, for the areas to be treated must also be clearly indicated.

6.25 On simple drawings where the areas are well defined and of uncomplicated shape it could, by shading the areas in light blue, be left to the photographer to do the masking and other preparation. (Fig **6.17**)

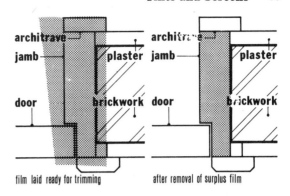

6.15 *When tint is laid over adjacent lettering prior to trimming, the adhesive layer can easily lift and damage the lettering as shown*

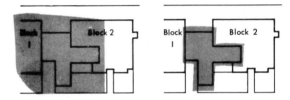

6.16 *To avoid accidental damage to adjacent lettering, and to economise on the tint, trim to the approximate shape of the area required before applying to the art work*

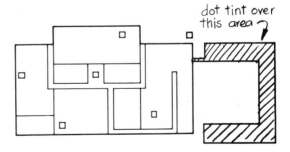

6.17 *Where the areas to be tinted are few and well defined simple shapes, they could be shaded in light blue and the instructions written on for the photographer to prepare the overlays*

6.26 While this may be done on occasions, to save time for example, it is not good practice. First, because of the additional production costs but secondly, and much more important, the loss of direct control over the positioning of the tints where two or more different patterns are to be laid on the same drawing. (Fig **6.18**)

6.27 The only really satisfactory way is to provide a separate translucent overlay for each different tint, with register marks for accurate positioning over the base drawing. The areas to be tinted would be masked out and the grade and density of the required tint written on. (Fig **6.21**)

6.28 The overlays should preferably be of a material not affected by atmospheric change, but be careful to match them with the base material so that differential movement between them is avoided. A drawing on board or film should have film overlays; a drawing on tracing paper should have overlays of tracing paper and so on.

6.29 Register marks should ideally be placed outside the drawing area but if this is not possible, then position them in an open space so that they cannot be mistaken for part of the illustration and so that they can be easily spotted out on the film intermediate. (Fig **6.19**)

6.30 Use at least three register marks to be certain that there can be only one position of the overlay to the base drawing. Do not make their design too elaborate as this could lead to a lot of unnecessary work; a simple cross should suffice. (Fig **6.20**) Remember that these marks are to assist the photographer in the accurate register-ing of one or more film positives so do not change the design. He will have enough to do without wondering what has happened to the marks he was just getting accustomed to using.

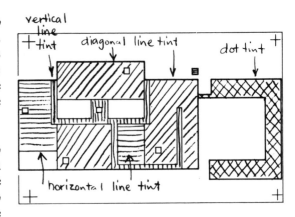

6.18 *When two or more different tints are required on the same drawing, the method described in Fig* **6.17** *can become very confusing*

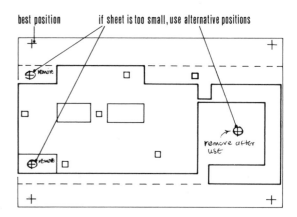

6.19 *Register marks should preferably be positioned well clear of the drawing area. If this is not possible then place them where they are obvious and can be easily removed after photography*

6.20 *Do not make the design of register marks too elaborate. With a lot of overlays and a minimum of three per overlay, you could make yourself a lot of unnecessary work*

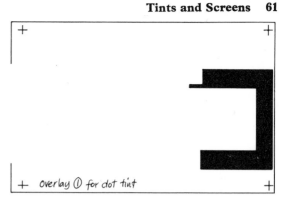

+ Overlay ① for dot tint

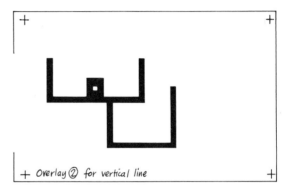

+ Overlay ② for vertical line

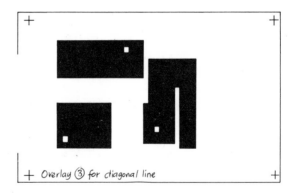

+ Overlay ③ for diagonal line

6.21 *This is how the drawing shown in Fig 6.18 should be treated. A separate overlay for each different tint all registered over the base drawing with the instructions clearly visible*

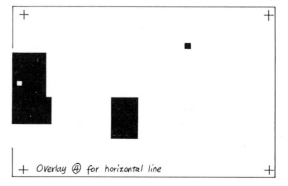

+ Overlay ④ for horizontal line

6.31 If several overlays are to be used on the same base drawing, graduate the size of the register marks so that the largest is on the base drawing and the smallest on the uppermost overlay. In this way the mark on the lower sheet can be seen extended beneath that of the next upper sheet, thus aiding accurate positioning both in the overlay preparation and photographic process. (Fig **6.22**)

6.32 Masking the area to be tinted can be carried out by painting on the overlay in solid black ink, paint or other photo-opaque colour, applying dry transfer light-fast sheets cut to size or using one of the masking films as the overlay itself, removing the light-fast layer except where the tint is required.

6.33 Specifying the grade and density of a dot or line tint is simply a matter of clearly indicating on each overlay the number of lines per inch and, where necessary, the percentage of solid black required. Remember that this time the tint is to be laid *after* reduction so that no allowance for the reduction need be made; therefore the screen the printer decided upon for the half-tone pictures is the maximum which should be specified, bearing in mind that the grade should not be too coarse.

6.34 Finally, do not use one overlay for two or more different tints. After photography the overlay appears black with a series of clear spaces where the tint is to go. (Fig **6.23**) The photographer will just want to lay a film grid over the whole overlay (not cut out little pieces to stick over the areas). With more than one tint on the same overlay, he will have to refer constantly to the original to see what goes where or make duplicates and spot out to form his own separate overlays. This can be very time-consuming and invites error so keep everything as straightforward as possible by making it a rule – one overlay, one tint.

Application by Hand
6.35 Adding tonal difference by hand must of necessity be restricted to line patterns for

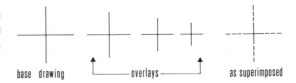

base drawing   overlays   as superimposed

6.22 *The register mark should be drawn so that it is largest at the base drawing and progressively smaller on each successive overlay, to assist in accurate positioning both before and after photography*

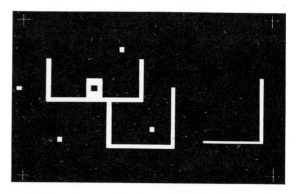

6.23 *How the overlay appears when ready for applying the film grid. If one tint only is required, it is a simple enough job to back it with the grid required. If more than one is needed then constant reference to the original drawing is necessary which, because of the probable difference in size, will be no easy task*

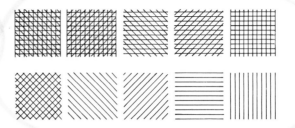

although dotting and other shading can be, and often are, applied successfully, the grade and density cannot be controlled and the variation between what should be similar patterns becomes too great to be acceptable.

6.36 This is not to say that the range of line patterns is not sufficient for general use. By combining line spacing and weight with vertical, horizontal and oblique forms, as many different patterns can be used as, for example, using dot tints. (Fig **6.24**)

6.37 Ruling by hand will take longer than either applying film tints or preparing an overlay, but nevertheless should not be condemned too hastily for, like all methods, it has advantages, and there will always be occasions where this form of application will be found useful.

6.38 Much of the time spent on this method is taken by measuring or pricking off the line spacing prior to ruling and erasing these marks afterwards. This time can be saved where a translucent base material has been used by sliding beneath it a sheet of line tint which is used as a tracing guide. By using each line (or every other one, two or three as desired) combined with various positions, the same sheet will give a very flexible range and can be used again and again. (Fig **6.25**)

6.39 One of the main advantages of hand ruling is that it can be used on very large drawings where printed film sheets are too small to be economically used and where overlays would be difficult to handle because of their size.

6.40 There is also the distinct advantage of having an illustration with no appendages in the form of pieces of film or overlays to be accidentally or carelessly lost in transit, with no instructions or specification to be misinterpreted, just one sheet upon which the tonal differences are guaranteed to be as visible as the basic drawing no matter what reduction is applied.

6.24 Some of the variations which can be obtained using the same line spacing and thickness

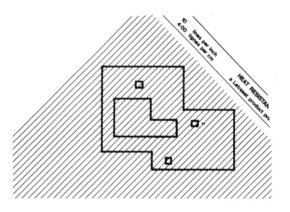

6.25 By using a sheet of line tint beneath the art work, tedious measuring and marking up are eliminated. The same sheet will provide all the horizontal, vertical and oblique variations, and can be used over and over again

Introduction

7.1 Lettering is arguably the most important part of any illustration. If the drawing itself is clear and easily understood then it should need no further addition than a caption. But if it is considered that explanatory notes are required, then it follows that the drawing could be obscure or even misleading without them and it also follows that such notes should be executed in a style that conforms to the basic principles of good lettering.

7.2 The most important principle is legibility which subsequently depends on (a) the form or shape of each character (Fig **7.1**), (b) the spacing of the characters in the formation of words and sentences (Fig **7.2**), (c) the spacing between lines of lettering (Fig **7.3**) and (d) the size of the characters.

7.3 Other factors which must be taken into account are that the style of lettering chosen should be appropriate to the illustration (i.e. a drawing expressing the rigid disciplines of an engineering subject should not be lettered in a decorative style) and that all notes should be as brief as possible without losing their informative content (i.e. do not use two words where one will do).

7.4 There are numerous ways of lettering illustrations, but for the scope of this book only hand, stencil, dry transfer and typeset methods are discussed in depth, being considered the most appropriate for general use, with a mention of the more exotic methods at the end of the chapter.

poor

better

7.1 *Legibility depends upon the form or shape of each character*

too wide

too close

better

7.2 *Legibility depends upon the spacing of the characters*

Hand Lettering

7.5 Hand lettering is becoming increasingly fashionable, not so much in the old established form of hand printing but rather as an extension of the illustrator's hand writing. (Fig **7.4**)

7.6 Main headings and perhaps sub-titles are usually lettered in a more conventional mechanical style, but notes and small informative blocks of lettering are executed in a freehand informal script which can enhance the illustration considerably.

7.7 Care must be taken to ensure that the style is consistent – do not change horses in midstream. And it must be clear and legible. Hand writing can be notoriously difficult to read, but when adapting it for notation it should be deliberately formed and not used as a quick and easy method of disposing of a chore. (Fig **7.5**)

7.8 The line thickness should be adequate for the proposed reduction to avoid a thin, spidery appearance and should ideally balance visually with the line work of the drawing. As a rule of thumb it should be about $1\frac{1}{2}$ times the thickness of the finest line used for the illustration.

7.9 Spacing when using hand lettering is less critical than with other methods, by reason of its informal nature. Provided that legibility is maintained, a rigid discipline of character and word spacing is unnecessary, perhaps even undesirable.

7.10 Horizontal alignment of sentences and consistent line spacing is however very important, and even the most casual style must conform to this rule. (Fig **7.6**)

too close

better

7.3 *Legibility depends upon the spacing between lines of lettering*

7.4 *Modern hand lettering tends towards an extension of the illustrator's hand writing*

7.5 *Hand lettering must be readable*

7.6 *Horizontal alignment is important even with a casual lettering style*

7.11 Hand lettering must have guide lines, but because of its flexible nature, whereby ascenders of lower-case letters can be shortened if they are likely to coincide with descenders, the somewhat rigid rules concerning line spacing, which must apply to the more mechanical forms, need not be followed, i.e. the lines of lettering may be closer together, thus saving space. (Fig **7.7**)

7.12 For the very informal style only the lower guide line need be drawn, while an even more simple method can be adopted when working on translucent materials. This entails the use of dry transfer line tint sheets of a suitable line spacing, which are positioned beneath the drawing eliminating the need for laborious marking out and drawing guide lines altogether. (Fig **7.8**)

7.13 It is difficult, indeed almost impossible, to hand letter for differing reductions and get a satisfactory final result. It is essential therefore, that all drawings to be hand lettered are prepared for the same reduction. If this cannot be done at the initial drawing stage, then the set can be matched up by obtaining photographic intermediate copies of the odd-sized drawings, enlarged or reduced as necessary, which are then lettered up and used as final art work.

7.14 Finally, remember that there is a limit to the size that the hand can easily accommodate. Do not attempt to letter in too large a size, for it will be difficult to keep the characters consistent in shape, the standard will fall and the advantage of speed will be lost. A capital height of 10 mm (Fig **7.9**) or lower-case 'x' height of 5 mm (Fig **7.10**) are quite large enough for comfort. Anything which requires a larger size should be reduced as a photographic intermediate and lettered as described above.

preformed anodised cover with h.w. plugs to p.c. cowil screed on roofing slabs

7.7 *Line spacing may be closer because of the flexible style*

dry transfer line tint sheet beneath as a lettering guide

chips to roof ay on roofing slab anodised cover preformed stri edge beams a cover plates anc

7.8 *Use of dry transfer line tint sheets to avoid the need for ruling guide lines*

10 mm

A B C D E F C

7.9 *A maximum capital height of 10 mm is large enough for freehand lettering*

5 mm

a b c d e f g h i j k l

7.10 *A maximum 'x' height of 5 mm is large enough for freehand lettering*

Stencil

7.15 Stencil lettering has the advantage of relative speed and simplicity depending upon the make and size of the stencil used, and the elimination of debate on suitable line thicknesses as these are strictly related to the size of stencil used.

7.16 The main disadvantage is that, apart from the somewhat limited 'microfilm' range, there is as yet no series where the character size and line thickness exactly relates over a large range of reductions. However, if the number of different reductions for the drawing set is limited and can be related to a suitable stencil range, then this method offers an efficient way of clearly representing notation.

7.17 The range of styles is limited at present to single-stroke forms (Fig **7.11**) though experiments have been made in a multi-thickness form which indicates a possible future breakthrough in this stencil style. (Fig **7.12**) At least the present available range almost entirely consists of the very useful three-in-one format.

7.18 Spacing stencil letters and figures can be difficult to judge and maintain because of the close proximity of the cut-out characters, necessary to restrict the overall length of the stencil to manageable proportions. (Fig **7.13**) Some of the coloured plastics can make this task even more difficult, especially if the cut is chamfered rather than vertical, which gives the illusion of a double image. (Fig **7.14**)

ABCDEGHIJKLMNOPQRSTUVWX

abcdefghijklmnopqrstuvwx

1234567890

STANDARDGRAPH

ABCDEFGHIJKLMNOPQ

abcdefghijklmnopqrstuv

1234567890

UNO ARCHITECTURAL

ABCDEGHIJKLMNOPQRSTUV

abcdefghijklmnopqrstuvwx

1234567890

FABER CASTELL

7.11 *Some of the range of stencils showing the limitations of the single stroke style*

the first stroke

after finishing

7.12 *Part of a multi-thickness form of experimental stencil*

GROUND FLOOR PLAN

GROUND FLOOR PLAN

G R O U N D F L O O R P

7.13 *Good and bad letter spacing*

7.19 Line spacing has to be carefully measured so that if an ascender and descender appear one immediately below the other, there is sufficient space between to prevent them touching. Such spacing can be judged by eye after some practice, avoiding the need to draw guide lines. A useful tip is to position the top of the lower case 'l' just clear of the bottom of a descender on the line above. (Fig **7.15**) This will ensure that all other characters, capitals and figures included, will also not touch. But be careful to allow the correct margin if there are no descenders on a particular line from which to measure.

7.20 Stencils which are produced for use with ball-point pen or pencil can be adapted for use with ink in a more informal style, though will have a more restricted use because of their tendency towards the larger sizes. The characters are first drawn in pencil and then traced in outline form in ink by hand or hatched or shaded as the drawing style allows. (Fig **7.16**)

Dry Transfer

7.21 Dry transfer lettering can be very tedious to use if there are many lengthy notes required, so before deciding on this method it is worth looking to see how much lettering is likely to be needed for the drawing set as a whole. Time may well dictate which method will be best.

7.22 Dry transfer hit the graphics scene with a resounding impact and remains a very strong competitor to other methods by reason of its ease (some better than others) of application, range of type styles, legibility and good reproduction qualities.

7.23 It is not the complete answer to the illustrator's lettering problems as may be first thought. It is not cheap; it is slow to apply; the range of sizes, though large, may not suit the reduction range you wish to work to. Provided, however, you are aware of the limitations and can plan your work accordingly, this method can give your illustrations that professional finish that few other systems can as easily provide. (Fig **7.17**)

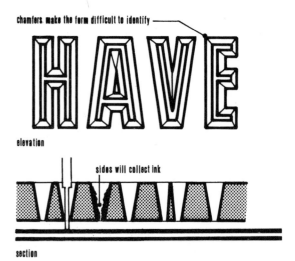

7.14 Section and elevation showing chamfered cut of character. Originally designed to facilitate the easy location of nib to character, in practice it is not helpful

7.15 To space lines by eye easily, position the top of the lower-case 'l' just below any descender on the line above. All subsequent characters can be lettered without fear of any overlapping

7.16 Stencils for pencil or ball-point pen can be adapted for ink work by tracing a pencil image in ink freehand

ABCDEFGH
abcdefghijk
1234567890

FOLIO MEDIUM EXTENDED

ABCDEFGHIJKL
abcdefghijklm
1234567890

GILL BOLD CONDENSED

ABCDEFGHIJKL
abcdefghijklm
1234567890

GROTESQUE 9

ABCDEFGHI
abcdefghijklm
1234567890

EUROSTYLE MEDIUM

ABCDEFGH
abcdefghijkl
1234567890

CENTURY SCHOOLBOOK BOLD

ABCDEFGHIJK
abcdefghijklmn
1234567890

PLANTIN BOLD CONDENSED

ABCDEFGH
abcdefghijklm
1234567890

TIMES BOLD

7.17 *Some of the large range of dry transfer styles*

ABCDEFGHIJI
abcdefghijklmr
1234567890

JENSON MEDIUM

7.24 Contrary to advertising claims, there is not a lot to choose between the various brands generally available. The basic materials are similar but with minor differences in the transfer letter thickness, colour and thickness of backing sheet and whether loose or attached, thickness of base carrier film, dust-proof adhesive or not and number of type faces and range of sizes in each style.

7.25 Regardless of make, however, they are all dry and they are all transferred in the same way. They will all be satisfactory within their own stated limitations so that, again, personal preference is the criterion of selection.

7.26 It is possible to damage the lettering even after burnishing, so care must be taken to prevent accidental damage when storing or carrying art work. It is generally heatproof and flexible but will not stand up indefinitely to rough treatment, so lettering should be the last job on any illustration.

7.27 If any tint is to be applied, do this before lettering, for even the clear carrier film will take away some of the denseness of the characters. Additionally, if the shading film has to be lifted for any reason, it will lift also the lettering you have carefully applied in exactly the same way as we use cellulose tape to remove unwanted characters. (Fig **7.18**)

7.28 If the brand of lettering has spacing marks then use them, especially when applying large lettering. (Fig **7.19**) Spacing large characters by eye is difficult and time consuming, but bad spacing of main headings and titles designed to attract attention will always look that much worse. The smaller sizes are much easier to handle and after practice can be successfully spaced by eye.

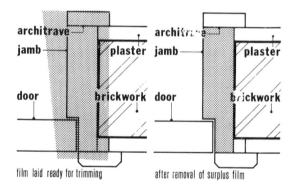

7.18 How dry transfer lettering can be damaged by accidental application of shading film

7.19 *Using spacing marks to set characters*

7.29 Line spacing must relate to the size of the lettering to avoid the possibility of ascenders and descenders overlapping. The closest line spacing to achieve this is equal to the point size of the lettering, so that 16 pt letters should be set on lines spaced 16 pts apart – in typographical terms, 'set solid'. (Fig **7.20**)

7.30 If it suits, lettering can be given more 'air' and set in lines further apart, for example 16 on 18 which is 16 pt lettering set 18 pts apart. Lettering specified by point size can thus be easily spaced using a depth scale (Fig **7.21**) and ruling faint blue lines on which to set the characters. Do not use pencil guide lines which will need to be erased, possibly taking your lettering with them. Blue lines will not reproduce and time will be saved by not having to erase them.

7.31 Lettering sized in millimetres presents a slight problem inasmuch as the height specified is usually that of the capital 'E', with no allowance for a lower-case descender. To ensure the correct line spacing, a capital and a lower-case character with a descender should be measured overall which will equal the 'set solid' or minimum line spacing for that size of lettering. (Fig **7.22**)

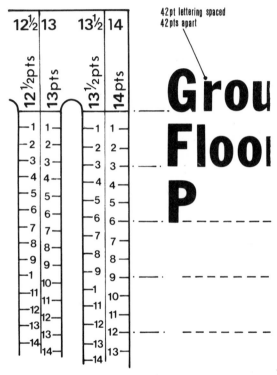

7.20 *Lettering set solid, i.e. the lines are spaced apart by the same number of points as the typeface size*

7.21 *Using the depth scale to set out lines of lettering and to determine the spacing of lettering already set*

7.22 *To determine the minimum spacing for lettering specified by cap height, set the capital 'e' alongside a lower-case letter with a descender such as a 'g' and measure the overall height · The resulting figure is the minimum line spacing for that particular style*

Typesetting

7.32 Typeset lettering can be a blessing inasmuch as the notes are 'ready-made' and just need mounting in position. The lettering is proofed up as reproduction (repro) copy either on a high quality clay-faced paper or as a photographic bromide. (Fig **7.23**)

7.33 In either case the lettering has to be cut out and fixed to the art work. As with dry transfer this can be tedious but, provided that the setting is accurate, must nevertheless be quicker than some other methods.

7.34 The notes must be carefully composed in the first instance so that after setting there should be no need to cut and reshape notes. (Fig **7.24**) This rearrangement of the typesetting is very slow work and too much of it will rapidly negate the 'whole note' advantage this method has.

7.35 It should also be remembered that repro copy is more substantial than translucent materials such as tracing paper, polyester film, etc. If it is to be affixed to such flexible material, a rigid backing must be provided to keep the art work flat, for excessive flexing will dislodge the copy. It is advisable, even with a rigid backing, to fix a protective sheet over the art work to prevent accidental damage or movement once the copy has been stuck down.

Other Methods

7.36 There are of course other methods of lettering, some of which do not easily lend themselves to easy application, others where the range of styles is too small, and still others which have yet to be fully developed.

THE WIDE CARRIAGE TYPEWRITER

7.37 This is somewhat cumbersome, and the drawing has also to be lifted from the drawing board to be lettered. To be efficient the notes should be typed not as separate blocks but all the first lines of each note from left to right across the drawing, then all the second lines and

7.23 *An example of reproduction copy pulled up by the printer for use as art work*

7.24 *The advantage of repro copy can be offset if the copy has to be cut and reshaped. The example has been mounted on a black background to show the intricate cutting that results when the copy is not set to the correct measure*

so on. It demands careful planning, for correction is not easy.

THE LETTERING MACHINE

7.38 This is an improvement inasmuch as it can be attached to a parallel motion unit or drafting machine scale. The drawing thus remains on the board and there is much more flexibility in the operation of the equipment. It has a keyboard which can provide a range of characters suitable for most purposes and can offer a choice of type sizes.

7.39 Other forms of lettering machine will produce, on translucent adhesive-backed tape, words which can be cut up and applied in dry transfer form to make up lines of notes as required. These words are produced from discs which carry the capitals, lower-case and numerals of a particular size and style. These discs are interchangeable to give a range which, though useful, is at present somewhat limited.

USE OF CARRIER FILM

7.40 The disadvantage of being able to set only one line at a time is avoided by having the notes photoset on a clear adhesive-backed carrier film which is cut and dry-transferred to the art work. The particular advantage of this method is that the notes are transferred complete in one stage and can be set in almost any typeface and size. The disadvantage is the comparatively high cost.

7.41 A cheaper alternative is to use a blank carrier film and the ordinary typewriter to letter the notes. The complete note can be transferred as described above, the style and size however cannot be varied beyond the scope of the typewriter used. The matt surface of the film will enable hand, stencilled and other lettering methods to be used if the additional work is considered justified by having the complete drawing notation available for trial positioning before final fixing.

Introduction

8.1 It is by no means certain that a set of illustrations will always be redrawn entirely. Indeed, it is very likely that among the author's copy will be some photographs and other half-tone pictures from catalogues or other published sources which may require some treatment in one way or another, but not necessarily redrawing.

8.2 So far only the ideal has been discussed, i.e. that of redrawing all the draft material to maintain consistency of style, but time and resources may dictate that some of the author's copy has to be used as final art work by the addition of some treatment.

8.3 This treatment may be minor or major and take the form of :
(1) Addition of linework and lettering by direct application or by overlay.
(2) Cutting and joining various parts of various pictures or drawings to form a new illustration.
(3) A combination of (1) and (2).

8.4 Due consideration still has to be given to line weight and lettering size to maintain some degree of consistency, but particular care should be taken when applying the treatment so that after photography the additions are as inconspicuous as possible.

Adaptation of Photographs

8.5 Photographs which have not been published are continuous tones inasmuch as the image has not been photographed through a grid or screen (necessary if the picture is to be reproduced). They can be adapted by the use of overlays or the addition of linework to extend the picture or by retouching. Half-tones, i.e. those which have been reproduced as screened

8.1 *The moiré (mwaray) or variegated effect obtained when two screens of different gauges are superimposed*

pictures, are more of a problem because they must be shot using the same screen otherwise they may clash causing what is known as a moiré effect. (Fig **8.1,** page 74)

8.6 Overlays can be used to add lines, lettering, hatching, etc., when such treatment cannot be applied direct because the photograph must not be marked or when the additions are required to be shot as a line over the half-tone picture, i.e. the additional work to be shown solid against a screen background. (Fig **8.2**) The new work is prepared on the overlay as a normal line drawing and subsequently stripped into the photograph either as solid black or reversed black-to-white as required.

8.7 Extending a photograph by adding line-work can apply to a tonal or line picture. An elevational shot of a subject can have a sectional line drawing added to show the outside and inside on the same illustration (Fig **8.3**) or a line picture may simply be extended line for line.

8.8 Retouching can be considerably more complex, involving perhaps the use of the air brush. In general it will only be found necessary to mask out unwanted areas of a picture, using a suitably marked up overlay or cut-out frame, or minor addition or obliteration using a medium-soft grade of pencil to match the light and dark shades of the photograph.

8.9 Finally, it is important to remember when dealing with any art work which is to be shot as a half-tone, that everything will 'show'. As will be seen later, a line shot can be subsequently treated to omit joins, patches, instructions, etc., but for half-tones much greater care is needed. You cannot conceal the edges of cut-out lettering or pictures that have been stuck down or any joints, creases or folds. The art work will usually be 'squared up', i.e. the picture will have a grey background giving it the appearance of being mounted on a board. (Fig **8.4**) Any instructions, identifying references, figure numbers etc. must be positioned outside this area.

8.2 *The upper example shows treatment added and shot as a half-tone. Below it is the same treatment stripped in solid on the half-tone*

Adaptation of Linework

8.10 Line diagrams which have already been published present much the same problems as do photographs, for the majority of such material is printed on glossy art paper which may not take an ink line very well. Additionally, they could be printed in a colour that will not easily reproduce, or against a background of solid colour that cannot be filtered out or in some other form equally difficult to deal with. Each illustration will have to be considered individually and the treatment decided upon carefully applied to match the style, weight and thickness of the existing linework.

8.11 When the treatment involves alteration as well as addition, it is best to use an overlay for the new work. Not only does this avoid the need to prepare the surface, should this be necessary, but it makes the masking or obliteration easier because no lines are required to be drawn over the treated areas. The art work should be mounted on fashion or art board to provide a stable backing to which the overlay can be attached.

8.12 When the art work only needs extending it should also be mounted on board but with a good drawing surface so that the new work can be drawn adjacent to the existing art work. When adding such linework always start next to the existing material and work away, never towards. (Fig **8.5**)

8.13 A lot of promotional material, advertisements, catalogues, etc., are printed in one or more colours, some of which may not reproduce because the shade is too light, or the lines may be reversed out in white. The treatment here may simply be to make such lines denser by tracing over in ink or pencil depending upon the surface of the paper. Try as far as possible to draw direct on to the art work, for the register of an overlay must be exactly right if it is to work and this is very difficult to accomplish. It would in fact be easier, if time permitted, to trace the whole illustration as new art work instead of using an overlay.

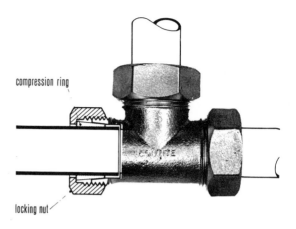

8.3 Linework can be added to a photograph to give more information

8.4 A typical 'squared-up' half-tone. The reduction has been marked on within the area in blue pencil but is still visible, as is the vertical crease

Cutting and Joining

8.14 This form of treatment can normally only be applied to art work which is to be shot as line and not half-tone. The latter can be used if a collage effect is desired or where the joins are not required to be invisible. It is not impossible to successfully join continuous tone prints to be used as half-tones but this depends greatly on the simplicity of subject and composition of the picture and should not be attempted unless some skill has been attained.

8.15 For line shots there is very little that cannot be attempted and a veritable patchworked piece of copy can usually give a satisfactory result. As with most treatments it should not be abused. Do not deliberately tempt fate with intricate marquetry which will need a lot of delicate spotting out after photography. Remember that at least half the skill needed to produce a good result comes from the photographer, so do not make his job unnecessarily difficult.

8.16 Cutting and joining should be restricted to flexible materials. Boards can be so treated but need to be mounted on a backing at least as thick as the art work to prevent the joints flexing, and this increases the handling difficulties. Backing boards must be used whatever material is to be joined, and the thickness will relate directly to the thickness of the original art work. The object is to prevent excessive flexing which may disturb the positioned pieces of copy, and as a rule, the thinner the art work the thinner may be the backing board within the prescribed limits.

8.17 For the best results, the made-up (or composite) art work should present a flat surface to the camera, i.e. the parts are either *all* placed on top of a backing sheet or board, are *all* inset into the backing sheet or *all* butt-jointed. (Fig **8.6**) Try to avoid a mixture of two or more of these methods to prevent the possibility of shadows being visible after photography. When insetting part of a picture into the backing sheet, a good joint is essential. Achieve this by placing the new art work in position on the backing and

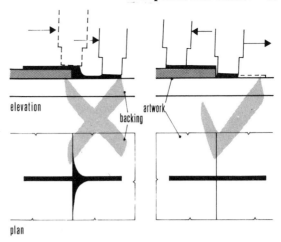

8.5 *Lines should always be drawn away from the edges of mounted art work to avoid the ink running into the vertical surface of the cut plane*

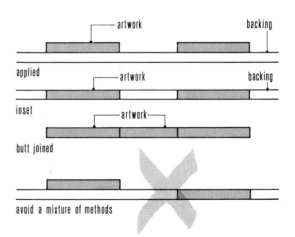

8.6 *The three methods of making up art work. The surfaces are irregular in height and preferably should not be mixed on the same illustration*

cutting through both at the same time. After discarding the unwanted part, the insertion can be taped or glued in the usual way.

Adhesives and Tapes

8.18 Fixing art work down can be by either of two basic methods – using adhesive or pressure-sensitive tape. Adhesives should themselves be of a flexible nature, that is to say that they should allow the art work to be moved after initial application so that the exact position can be more easily found. There are many suitable types available, ranging from wax-based, aerosol sprays of various kinds to latex cement in tins and tubes.

8.19 Do not use an adhesive that is too strong for the material you require to paste down, or one that is too wet which will cause the thinner materials to wrinkle. Ideally, it should hold the art work in position but also enable it to be lifted, if necessary, and remounted, and be transparent when dry.

8.20 The adhesive should be applied to the whole of the art work, not just a dab at each corner, in order to gain a flat surface with maximum overall adhesion. (Fig **8.7**) The backing should be rigid enough to prevent excessive flexing which will cause lifting and creasing of the art work.

8.21 Almost any adhesive tape can be used to fix down art work depending on the particular situation. If the tape will be well clear of any part of the drawing, then any opaque, light-fast, masking as well as clear tape can be used, for the image it leaves after photography can easily be spotted out. If the tape has to be placed over any part of the drawing, then a translucent matt- or glossy-surfaced type must be used. Matt-surfaced tape is best when ink or pencil has to be drawn over a join but if only the glossy cellulose type is available, the surface can be rubbed with an ink eraser which will provide a perfectly satisfactory finish that will accept both ink and pencil.

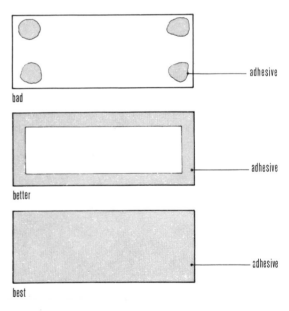

8.7 *Adhesive should be applied to achieve a flat surface with maximum adhesion*

8.22 If the art work is to be fixed to the face of a backing board then the tape must be applied all round its perimeter. (Fig **8.8**) If any gaps are left there is the chance of something sliding beneath and either lifting or tearing the art work. The tape must also be applied carefully so that there is no distortion and the art work remains perfectly flat. .

8.23 When the art work is to be butt-jointed, then the tape can be positioned on the face or on the reverse of the art work or on both. The choice is largely a personal one but one or two factors may influence the final decision:
(1) When there is no treatment to be applied over the joint, the tape is best on the back as there is then no raised surface to cause shadows.
(2) If treatment has to be applied over the joint, the tape should be on the face to prevent ink running between the edges of adjoining art work.
(3) If the edges of art work do not exactly butt together, the tape should be applied to both sides to avoid the adhesive on the tape being exposed on one side or another, attracting dirt which is extremely difficult to remove. (Fig **8.9**)

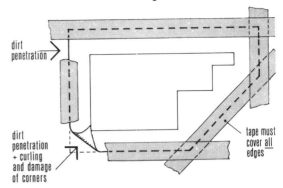

8.8 *Tape should be applied to all edges of the art work to prevent anything sliding between it and the backing*

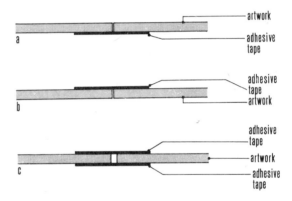

8.9 (a) *With no treatment required over the joint, the tape should be on the back only*
(b) *When treatment is required, put the tape on the face*
(c) *To cover any gaps between side joints, the tape should be on the face* and *the back*

Notes

Notes

Notes